DEATH & LIGHTHOUSES ON THE GREAT LAKES

DEATH & LIGHTHOUSES ON THE GREAT LAKES

A HISTORY OF MURDER AND MISFORTUNE

DIANNA HIGGS STAMPFLER

Published by The History Press
Charleston, SC
www.historypress.com

First published 2022

Manufactured in the United States

ISBN 9781467149952

Library of Congress Control Number: 2021950505

Notice: The information in this book is true and complete to the best of our knowledge. It is offered without guarantee on the part of the author or The History Press. The author and The History Press disclaim all liability in connection with the use of this book.

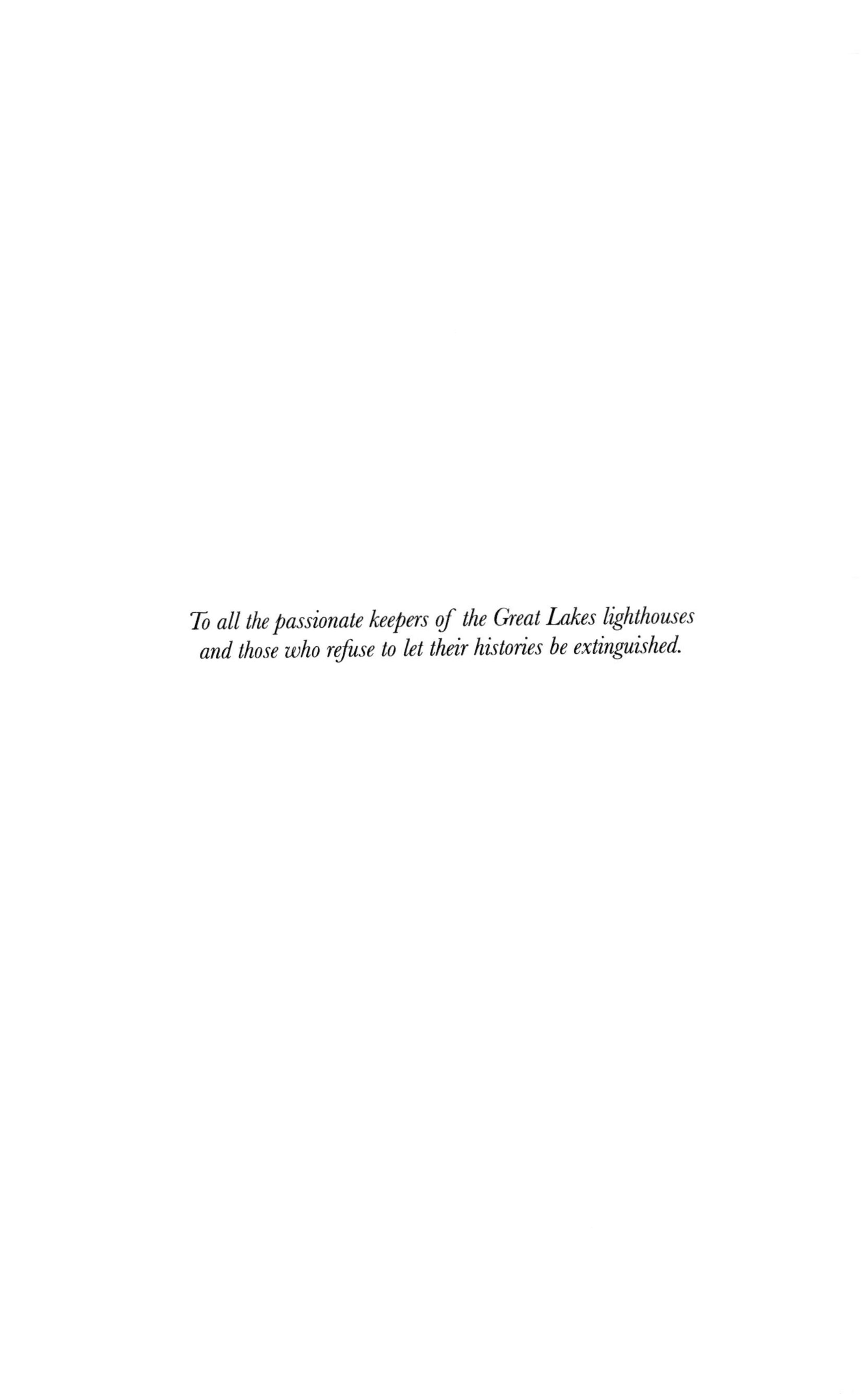

*To all the passionate keepers of the Great Lakes lighthouses
and those who refuse to let their histories be extinguished.*

DEATH & LIGHTHOUSES ON THE GREAT LAKES

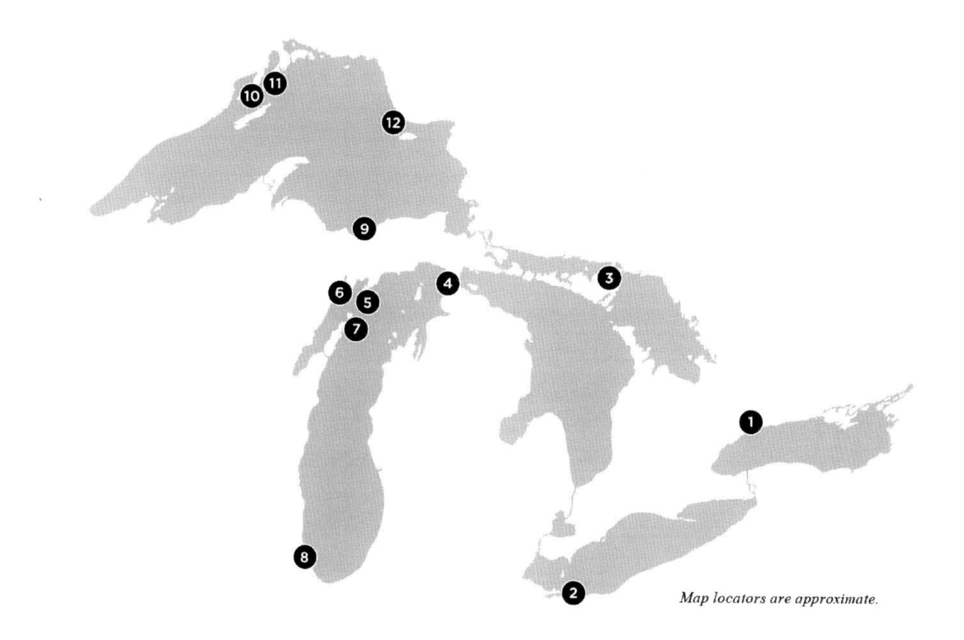

LAKE ONTARIO

1. Gibraltar Point Lighthouse

LAKE ERIE

2. South Bass Island Lighthouse

LAKE HURON

3. Clapperton Island Lighthouse

LAKE MICHIGAN

4. St. Helena Island Lighthouse
5. Poverty Island Lighthouse
6. Sand Point Lighthouse
7. Pilot Island Lighthouse
8. Grosse Point Lighthouse

LAKE SUPERIOR

9. Grand Island Lighthouse
10. Pie Island Lighthouse
11. St. Ignace Lighthouse
12. Michipicoten Island Lighthouse

CONTENTS

PREFACE

Losing one's life while tending to a Great Lakes lighthouse—or any navigational beacon anywhere in the world, for that matter—was, sadly, not such an unusual occurrence. The likelihood of drowning while at sea or being injured while on the job (ultimately leading to death) was often high in the late nineteenth and early twentieth centuries.

Death by murder, suicide or other graphic means was rarer but not unheard of. More than a dozen lighthouse keepers around the Great Lakes met their maker at the hands of others—by arson, poisoning, bludgeoning or other unknown means. A handful of these keepers, either because of depression, loneliness or fear, took their own lives. We may never know the true story of a few, as the deaths—now one hundred or more years old—weren't subjected to the forensic scrutiny and documentation that such crimes are given today.

I was reading Loren Graham's book *Death at the Lighthouse: A Grand Island Riddle* (Arbutus Press, 2013) about the 1908 deaths of head keeper George A. Genry and his assistant, Edward S. Morrison, when I started to wonder about who else had died mysteriously or tragically at their respective lighthouses. What were the stories behind those deaths? So, to Google I went.

A few cases were already familiar to me—most notably the death of Mary Terry, the keeper of the Sand Point Lighthouse in Escanaba in 1886. I was also aware of the suicides of George Sheridan (the son of the South Manitou Sheridans) at Grosse Point Lighthouse in Evanston, Illinois, in 1915 and William Prior (the father of George Prior, his assistant) at the Big Bay

Point Lighthouse near Marquette in 1902 (both featured in my first book, *Michigan's Haunted Lighthouses*, The History Press, 2019).

Given that most of my historical research and writing over the years has been focused on my home state of Michigan, I decided to broaden my scope for this book to include stories from throughout the entire Great Lakes region, from Minnesota to New York and even Canada. And while the number of tales was limited, the details were numerous, often obscure and sometimes inconclusive as to the ultimate cause of death. Most of the stories in this book are new to me, making my research much more methodical but also prompting my travel to areas I'd never visited before (like South Bass Island, Grand Island and the waters alongside Door County, Wisconsin's Pilot Island).

As always, I wanted to know more than what I could find on Google—more than what has already been shared by others. I wanted to delve into old newspaper articles (which were often contradictory), gather death records, look for historic photographs, visit cemeteries and dig further into not only the stories but also the lives of those who died in such tragic ways.

Since I had honed my skills while researching for my first book, I quickly logged into Newspapers.com, Ancestry.com, FamilySearch.org and Michiganology.com (formerly SeekingMichigan.org), as well as the websites for the National Archives, Library of Congress, United States Lighthouse Society and U.S. Coast Guard and various city, township, county and library websites for nuggets of information.

I also sent countless emails to others who had written about unfortunate keeper deaths and read books by fellow authors in search of answers. One of the most memorable trips I made was to Columbus, Ohio, to visit the library archives at Ohio State University, followed by a visit to the former Toledo State Hospital (and its adjacent cemetery) where I found detailed documents and official lighthouse records about the three keepers who died (at different times) at the South Bass Island Lighthouse.

To some, my interest in murder, suicide and death may seem a bit strange or even questionable. Admittedly, it is often concerning to even myself. Growing up in the generation that watched shows like *Law & Order*, *Forensic Files*, *Snapped*, *Unsolved Mysteries*, *Criminal Minds* and the like, I have developed an interest in such topics, and for years, I've researched various aspects of "dark tourism" in Michigan and around the world.

I've also found inspiration among the pages of books by true crime authors (and fellow "Michigangsters") Tobin Buhk, Mardi Link, Fred Stonehouse and Jenn Carpenter, who recently opened up a bookstore in Lansing's REO

Town called Deadtime Stories dedicated to this genre (next to Jenn's other unique retail store, The Screamatorium).

It is an interesting hobby to say the least. But I know I'm not alone in my fascination, and in that, I (oddly) find comfort. Thankfully, my devoted "partner in crime" not only embraces my quest to learn more about these macabre stories but also willingly drives me to various locales to research and take photographs as necessary (although I sometimes detect a slight rolling of the eyes).

ACKNOWLEDGEMENTS

As always, thank you to my parents and grandparents, who instilled in me a love of history, traveling and storytelling; my children, who continue to indulge me in my passion for all things Michigan and the Great Lakes; and Greg, who never (or rarely) complains about visiting lighthouses, cemeteries and other historic sites in the name of my research.

INTRODUCTION

The Great Lakes region boasts over 3,200 miles of freshwater shoreline (more if you circle every island within the five individual lakes: Ontario, Erie, Huron, Michigan and Superior). These waterways were home to early Natives, well before French voyageurs began exploring this area.

According to the National Archives (Archives.gov):

> *Prior to 1789, during the colonial period, each colonial government determined the need for a lighthouse in their colony, financed its construction, and oversaw its operation. Twelve colonial lighthouses remained in the hands of the individual states throughout the period of confederation with additional lighthouses being erected. On August 7, 1789, President George Washington signed the ninth act of the U.S. Congress (1 Stat. 53), which provided that the states turn over their lighthouses, including those under construction and those proposed, to the central government. In creating the U.S. Lighthouse Establishment* [in 1792], *aids to navigation became the responsibility of the secretary of the treasury.*

An act of Congress, approved on August 31, 1852, transferred the administration of these lights from the Treasury Department to the United States Lighthouse Board, giving it the directive to maintain the growing number of lighthouses and navigational aids. Between 1903 and 1910, the governing organization of the lights was the Department of Commerce and Labor, Lighthouse Board. By 1910, responsibility for the lights was again redelegated—this time to the Lighthouse Service, under the Department of Commerce. It was during this period (June 1918) that keepers and employees finally qualified for retirement and disability (the first civil service to gain such benefits). On July 1, 1939, the U.S. Coast Guard was placed in charge of the lights, a role it maintains to this day.

The first lighthouse built along this expansive Great Lakes coastline was Gibraltar Point in Toronto, erected in 1808. This towering beacon on the bank of Lake Ontario remains as one of the most historic and iconic structures in that Canadian town.

Many early lighthouse keepers in the Great Lakes region were military veterans. At least one served in the Revolutionary War or the War of 1812, but most were former Civil War soldiers. In some cases, these men were wounded during combat, but that didn't stop them from performing the arduous job of tending to their lights.

There were many families who dedicated their lives to lighthouse keeping—most notably the Marshall family from the Straits of Mackinac area. Over the course of a century, they had at least twelve men (brothers, sons, fathers and grandsons) who tended an equal number of lights in Michigan for a cumulative three-hundred-plus years. Of those, at least two lost their lives while carrying out their duties, and one was institutionalized for years as a result of an on-the-job injury.

Other noteworthy families included the Sheridans (two generations between South Manitou Island and Kalamazoo River Light in Saugatuck, no longer standing) and the Bakers (three generations at Clapperton Island in Lake Huron), who collectively claim a variety of tragic deathly tales.

An unofficial assistant keeper on South Bass Island in Lake Erie, Ohio, was said to have committed suicide for fear of catching smallpox during the 1898 pandemic that swept through that state (ironic given the world situation in 2020–21), while another keeper slit his own throat in a remote island lighthouse off of Door County Peninsula in Wisconsin, the suspected result of a broken heart.

The keeper who stands above the rest is Mary Terry, who served eighteen years at the Sand Point Lighthouse in Escanaba in Michigan's Upper Peninsula. Appointed after her keeper husband died (before the light was even put into operation), Mary was a one-woman show until a suspicious fire claimed her life in 1886. To this day, no one can say for certain if her death was an accident or something more nefarious. A handful of other keepers died as the result of suspected criminal activities, although rarely were the culprits identified, caught or brought to justice.

In the pages of *Death & Lighthouses on the Great Lakes: A History of Murder & Misfortune*, you'll find an amalgamation of facts and theories, media coverage and historical documentation that brings these true crime stories to life—despite the deaths of those mentioned. Some stories are darker than others, but they are all tragic and sad in their own way.

If you have a deathly Great Lakes lighthouse story to share, please email Travel@PromoteMichigan.com.

PART I.

LAKE ONTARIO

1
GIBRALTAR POINT LIGHTHOUSE
TORONTO ISLANDS, CANADA

The oldest standing lighthouse on the Great Lakes—one of the oldest structures in Toronto—harbors a dark story tied to the tragic death of its first keeper.

In 1803, the Parliament of Upper Canada (today, the parts of Ontario that touch the Great Lakes shoreline) authorized the construction of the province's first three lighthouses, including one on Gibraltar Point in York (the original name for Toronto).

The *Maritime History of the Great Lakes* (MaritimeHistoryoftheGreatLakes.ca) notes that on March 16, 1808, the *Upper Canada Gazette* announced, "It is with pleasure we inform the public that the dangers to vessels navigating Lake Ontario will in a great measure be avoided by the erection of a lighthouse on Gibraltar Point, which is to be completed in compliance with an address of the house of assembly to the lieutenant governor."

Built of limestone that was brought over from the Queenston Quarry near Niagara River by the *Mohawk*, the original hexagonally shaped Gibraltar Point Light was fifty-two feet tall (today, it stands at sixty-two feet).

"Yes, just a landmark, but the landmark of all the landmarks, for it is the first and only example of stone and mortar, the first structure that remains intact of the skill of the pioneers who used the twenty-four-inch gauge, the common gavel and the chisel the stonemasons and their helpers the stone-setters and mortar mixers," wrote John Robertson in his 1908 book titled *Landmarks of Toronto*.

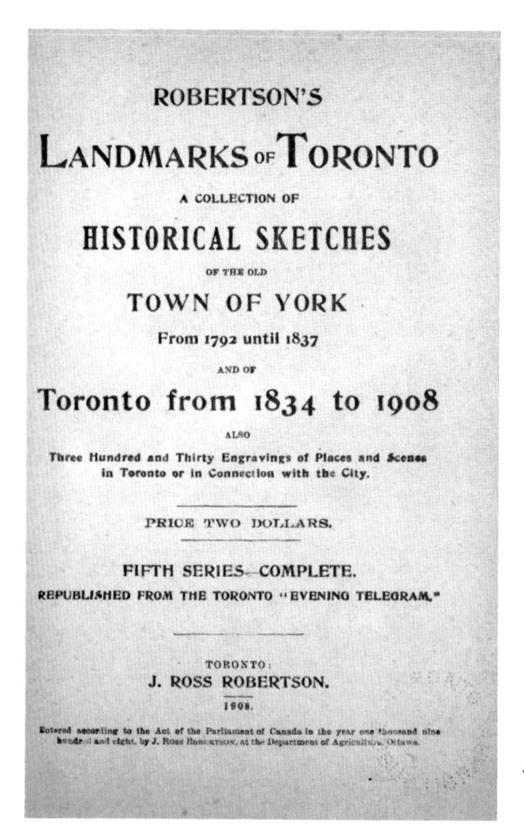

ROBERTSON'S

LANDMARKS OF TORONTO

A COLLECTION OF

HISTORICAL SKETCHES

OF THE OLD

TOWN OF YORK

From 1792 until 1837

AND OF

Toronto from 1834 to 1908

ALSO

Three Hundred and Thirty Engravings of Places and Scenes in Toronto or in Connection with the City.

PRICE TWO DOLLARS.

FIFTH SERIES—COMPLETE.

REPUBLISHED FROM THE TORONTO "EVENING TELEGRAM."

TORONTO:

J. ROSS ROBERTSON.

1908.

Entered according to the Act of the Parliament of Canada in the year one thousand nine hundred and eight, by J. Ross Robertson, at the Department of Agriculture, Ottawa.

In 1908, John Robertson shared details of the life and death of Gibraltar Point Lighthouse keeper John Paul "J.P." Radelmüller in his book *Landmarks of Toronto. From* Landmarks of Toronto, *public domain.*

John Paul "J.P." Radelmüller (also printed as Rademuller, Rademiller, Rattelmullar, Radan Muller, Muller and Miller) was the first keeper of the Gibraltar Point Light, appointed in the summer of 1809. Robertson noted this keeper was of German descent and was "a quiet, inoffensive man, who attended to his duties faith fully [*sic*]."

Radelmüller's upbringing and professional background was interesting, and thanks to a seven-page handwritten letter cataloged at the Library and Archives Canada (and transcribed on the blog 1812andallthat.wordpress.com by Eamonn O'Keeffe in 2016), we know in his own words the details that ultimately lead him to Gibraltar Point. The letter was written on January 1, 1808, and addressed to William Halton, the private secretary to Sir Francis Gore, lieutenant governor of Upper Canada. Full of phonetic spellings, misspellings, irregular capitalizations and obscure punctuation, the letter was part resume, part pleading, as Radelmüller fell on the mercy of others in a foreign land to provide what his past employers promised but never delivered.

Around 1763, Radelmüller was born in the German town of Anspach (in the province of Franconia). This was also where Queen Caroline, the wife of England's King George II, hailed from. It was an ironic connection, as Radelmüller would come to be in the employ of the royal family at the age of nineteen.

> *In the Year 1782, the 25th of Septr, I had the Honor to become a Servant to H.R. Highness the Duke of Gloucester* [Prince William Henry, King George III's brother] *in the character as Chamber Hussar in which service and station I remained until 1798. I gave up that servis for no other reason than my passialty for farmering, and of course was also desirous to see my relations and country again after so many years absence....After a few months stay, I return'd a gain to old England. As it happened that H.R. Highness the Duke* [of] *Kent* [Prince Edward Augustus, fourth son of King George III and for whom Canada's Prince Edward Island is named] *came home at the same time from America, I had the honor soon after his arrival to engage myself with him as porter, but, not long after that, H.R.H. was appointed commander-in-chief of British North American &c, as I was an old travelor, I got the charge of the package.*

This meant Radelmüller was in charge of gathering, wrapping, packing, bundling and arranging for transport all of the duke's belongings—from uniforms and toiletries to home furnishings and more—for the trip to Canada. But the two wouldn't make the trip alone on July 25, 1799. In addition to other servants, they were in the company of Theresa-Bernardine Mongenêt, who went by the name Madame Julie de St. Laurent. She was the duke's mistress. She was said to have been seven years older than he was, the wife of a French army colonel and not of royal blood, meaning the duke could not legally marry her, even if she hadn't already been espoused. She was also believed to be a prostitute, which clearly didn't sit well in the royal family.

The duke and his entourage boarded the HMS (Her Majesty's Ship) *Arethusa* in Portsmouth, Great Britain, on July 25, 1799, and set sail for Halifax. The trip lasted about forty-three days.

As was written on page 29 of the 234-page transcript *Wave to Whisper: British Military Communications in Halifax and the Empire, 1780–1880* by James H. Morrison (1979), "The ship HMS *Arethusa* was sighted on Friday, September 6, 1799, by the Sambro signal station. The word was sent to the Citadel that Prince Edward was aboard."

Among those who were dockside to welcome the passengers was Sir John Wentworth, the governor of Nova Scotia, who offered up his lodge on Bedford Basin to the lovebirds as their Canadian abode. Radelmüller and the rest of the staff ran the house as well as the social activities of the duke and his "French lady," as she was often called. It is said that this royal love affair went on for nearly thirty years before the duke and Julie parted ways and he married an appropriate English woman who could birth an heir to the throne.

> *His Royal Highness Staid* [stayed] *one year at Halifax; before he left that place, he inquired if there were any in his family, that should be desirous to settle in this country, and asked me if I am one of them. I answered him in the affirmative, His R.H.'s well known that I wished to have land, he offered me his assistance for some without my asking for any, and were I wished to have it if there should be any vacant. I thank'd him for the kind offer, and as I soon found out some vacant land not far from Halifax, which was ones designd for an officier, but happen'd to die before he located it, by this it remain'd vacant, which said land consisted of 1,000 acres more or less, I took the liberty to inform H.R.H.'s of the aforesaid land. He said as I had served so many years in the family, faithfully, he thinks me worthy of it, and will help me to get it. Besides this his R Highness was pleas'd to propose a place for me under government, as far my abilitys would admit, of which I was to take procession, as well as the foresaid land as soon he had left Halifax. But as the person who he had chosen for the care of his package, fell very ill short before His R.H. want to set off; for which reason H.R.H. desired with me to go with him to England, and he would give me free passage out again the spring following.*

Feeling an obligation to the duke, Radelmüller returned to England with him for a period of one year. And true to his word, the duke made sure that his faithful servant was allowed to return back to Canada the following spring. At this point, Radelmüller found employment as a steward for none other than Sir John Wentworth, who had provided his house for the duke the year prior, a position he held for a little over two years.

"I did not leave that place out of dislike, for I must confess I found His Excellency a very just and good governor, but, as I had left the servis of two royal princes, on account as I begin to get in years, to [retire] a little before I die."

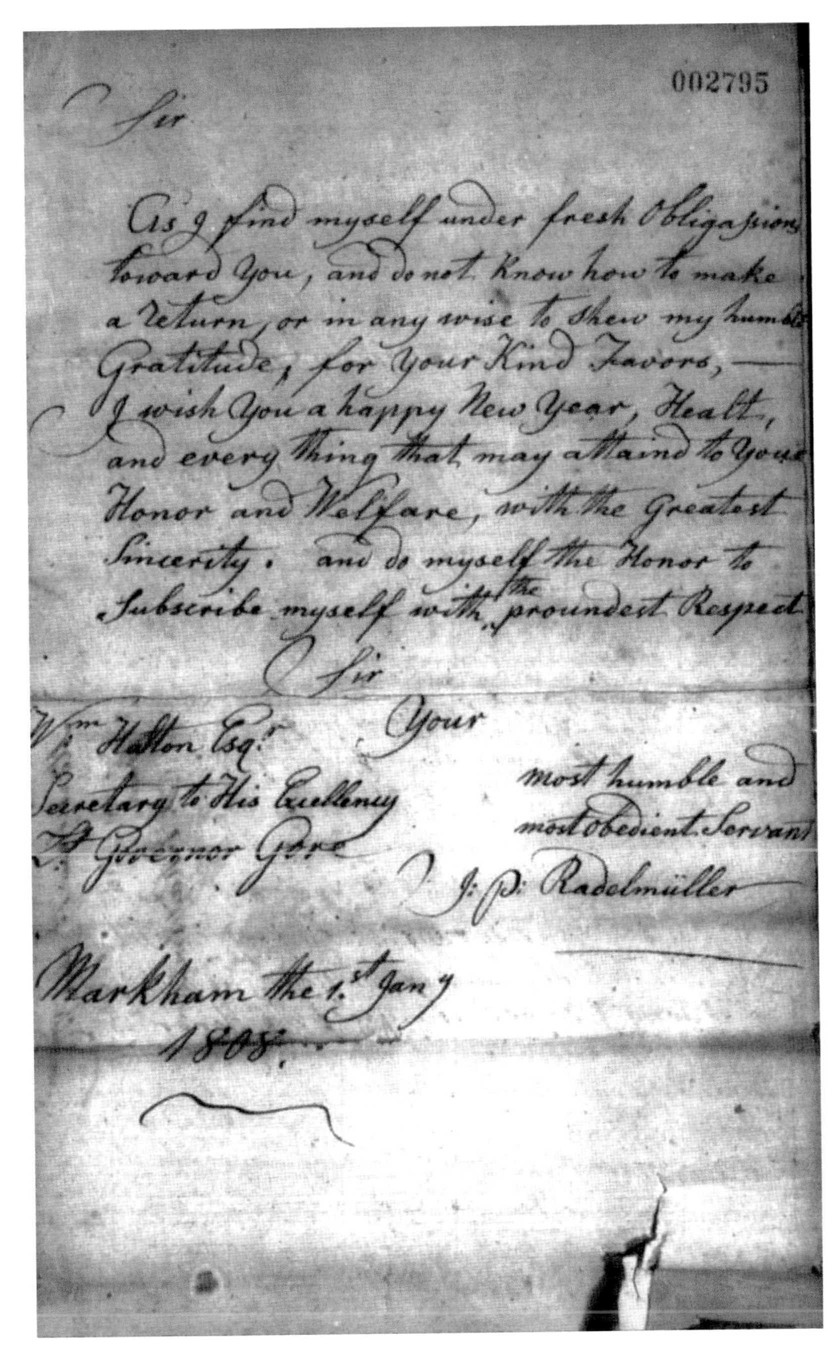

002795

Sir

As I find myself under fresh Obligassions toward You, and do not Know how to make a Return, or in any wise to shew my humble Gratitude, for Your Kind Favors, — I wish You a happy New Year, Healt, and every thing that may attaind to Your Honor and Welfare, with the Greatest Sincerity. and do myself the Honor to Subscribe myself with the proundest Respect

Sir

Your

most humble and most Obedient Servant

J: P: Radelmüller

Wm Halton Esqr
Secretary to His Excellency
Lt Governor Gore

Markham the 1st Jany 1808.

The final page of Radelmüller's January 1, 1808 letter to William Halton, the private secretary to Sir Francis Gore, lieutenant governor of upper Canada. *Courtesy of the Library and Archives Canada.*

Radelmüller was still in search of his own land, as he was anxious to begin farming. Yet, being a German by way of England in Halifax, it was helpful to have the support and endorsement of his previous employer to do so, especially when that person was the governor of Nova Scotia who had committed to providing the necessary letters and documentation that Radelmüller requested and required.

On November 23, 1803, six months after giving his notice, Radelmüller loaded all his belongings aboard a ship headed to the province of Upper Canada and anxiously awaited Wentworth's arrival with the ever-important paperwork. Imagine his disappointment—and likely anger—when Wentworth showed up that day empty-handed. Then Radelmüller was left to his own devices to make his way in another new region of Canada and hope for the best.

Instead of setting up a farmstead in Markham (less than twenty miles north of Toronto), Radelmüller found a new profession. According to O'Keeffe's website, "Radelmüller served as an interpreter for the German community in Upper Canada and established a school to teach English to the children of these settlers." Also, while in this area, "he penned the German translation of an 1806 government-sponsored agricultural tract encouraging farmers to cultivate hemp for export to Britain, where it was used to make rope for the Royal Navy." He apparently spent a little over a week in York, working with the printer on the project, for which he was paid £4 6s. (approximately $7.60 at the time or about $173 today).

Radelmüller's next profession would be his last. On July 24, 1809, Lieutenant Governor Francis Gore appointed him keeper of the newly established lighthouse at Gibraltar Point, and he moved into a small cottage beside the light to begin his tenure at the first permanent lighthouse on the Great Lakes.

The following spring, on March 20, 1810, Radelmüller married Magdalena (Burkholder) in Toronto's first church, St. James, located at the intersection of King and Church Streets (where St. James's Cathedral now stands). Their young daughter Arabella Ann was born in 1811.

In addition to raising his new family and tending the lighthouse, the German-born Radelmüller had a natural propensity for beer—brewing, drinking and selling it—with some going as far as to call him a bootlegger. "Muller, true to the customs of his fatherland, always liked a glass of beer, and by way of improving his stipend as lighthouse keeper, he always kept a spare keg on hand for his friends," Robertson wrote (1908, 382–83). "It is understood that the beer was obtained from a brewery near Lewiston, N.Y."

But not all supported the theories that Radelmüller was involved in the illegal sale of beer or other alcohol during his time at the light. Author Edward Butts noted in his book *Murder: Twelve True Stories of Homicide in Canada* (Butts 2011, 19), "It would seem to have been quite out of character for Radelmüller to have engaged in such activities. Moreover, if he were caught smuggling, it would have cost him his position as lightkeeper."

Additionally, given that his service occurred during the War of 1812, it seems unlikely that boats transporting illegal booze would have made it across the international waterway without being spotted (and subsequently detained) by patrolling warships. It was more likely that, given his remote locale at the lighthouse, he served as his own brewmaster, which would have also eliminated any additional cash expenditures involved in buying alcohol from others across the lake.

Regardless, if Radelmüller brewed or bought the beer to sell to local residents and soldiers, it certainly caused big trouble for him—ultimately leading to his demise.

The January 14, 1815 issue of the *York Gazette* noted: "Died on the evening of the 2nd of January, J.P. Radelmüller, keeper of the lighthouse of Gibraltar Point. From circumstances there is moral proof of his having been murdered. If the horrid crime admits an aggravation when the inoffensive and benevolent character of the unfortunate sufferer are considered, his murder will be pronounced most barbarous and inhuman. The parties lost with him are the proposed perpetrators and are in prison."

There are a half dozen (or more) varying accounts of what transpired after dark on Monday, January 2, 1815, to the fifty-two-year-old Radelmüller. The most far-fetched story claims that he was murdered, dismembered and buried in various locations around the lighthouse, never to be seen again. While that scenario is unlikely, it was known for certain that he died a violent death.

The object he was struck and killed with varies depending on which source you believe. Was it a metal belt buckle? A piece of firewood? It was possibly a shovel, which would have come in handy when burying body parts—if you subscribe to that theory.

And what was the motive behind the act of violence? Did Radelmüller cut off his guests after they overconsumed and became inebriated? Was he caught diluting the booze with water, thus reducing its potency while still trying to sell it at full price? Did someone simply attempt to steal the beer, and when Radelmüller fought back, was he attacked and subsequently killed?

Historian Eamonn O'Keeffe has extensively researched the Gibraltar Point Lighthouse in Toronto, built in 1808 and tended by John Paul "J.P." Radelmüller before his brutal murder in 1815. *Courtesy of Eamonn O'Keeffe.*

Or maybe it was something totally different. Who really knows?

A 2019 post on a subreddit for the discussion of "Canadian Myths, Legends, Unresolved Mysteries" shared a detailed account that seemed to fuel the more obscure theories that have been repeated and enhanced over the years.

> *John Paul couldn't fulfill an order placed by the two soldiers, so he cut the bootleg alcohol with water to fill out the difference. It was still freezing cold outside, and after the soldiers had purchased the alcohol, they headed back to their outpost, and on the way, were drinking from the bottles provided. The weather was so cold that the open bottles started to freeze, but as most know, alcohol has a much lower freezing point than water. The soldiers knew this; they became enraged, feeling like they'd been cheated and, being already drunk off the watered-down alcohol, headed back to the lighthouse. Radelmüller refused to give them their money back, and the soldiers broke*

> *down the door, shooting him dead on the thirteenth step (I might be wrong about which step—it was a long time ago that I heard this story) and then hacking him to pieces and burying him off site.*

Once again playing devil's advocate, Butts addresses some key issues in the infamous story that have been lost to time. "There are several problems with these rather melodramatic accounts," he wrote in his book (Butts 2011, 20). "Where were Magdalena and Arabella? Would intoxicated soldiers have been capable of carving up a body and scattering the parts in secret burial places? Considering it was January, the ground was probably frozen solid: would these secret burial places have been at all possible?" And furthermore, "There is no surviving record of just how the people of York became aware of the murder."

Records from 1815 are hard to come by, especially those of legal nature, but it was known that two Irish-born soldiers, John Blueman (also printed Blowman) and John Henry, were eventually arrested and charged with the keeper's death. These men were serving in the Glengarry Light Infantry, a unit that saw heavy action during the War of 1812, and were likely stationed at the blockhouse on Gibraltar Point, which guarded the mouth of York's harbor at nearby Fort York. Built in the late eighteenth or nineteenth century by the British army and Canadian militia troops, Fort York's mission was to defend and protect the settlement and the new capital of the Upper Canada region from the threat of military attack, primarily from the newly independent United States.

It took more than two months for the case against Blueman and Henry to come before Chief Justice Thomas Scott, and the trial took place in late March of that year. In his online post "New Light on Toronto's Oldest Cold Case," O'Keeffe notes that Blueman and Henry both pleaded not guilty to the charges facing them.

"The prosecution called seven witnesses, including David Thomson, a forefather of the billionaire Thomson media family and a mason who helped rebuild Fort York. Coroner Thomas Cooper also testified, filling in for his businessman father, William, the official coroner for the Home District," O'Keeffe wrote. "At least three and probably four other crown witnesses were privates of the Glengarry Light Infantry, presumably summoned to give evidence on the actions or whereabouts of Blueman and Henry on January 2nd." Interestingly, Magdalena never testified during the trial.

Trying a case with limited evidence was difficult, and the two men were acquitted of all charges. The *York Gazette* reported on April 15, 1815, "No conviction of the supposed murderers of the late J.P. Radelmüller."

This illustration of the Gibraltar Point Lighthouse was originally printed in *Robertson's Landmarks of Toronto* (vol. 2, page 203) by J. Ross Robertson, published in six volumes from 1893 to 1914. *From* Landmarks of Toronto, *public domain.*

Decades later, the stories and legends of what really happened to Radelmüller remained a topic of conversation—especially among those who tended the light in the years since his disappearance. John Robertson continued his account in *Landmarks of Toronto* (1908, 383).

"This is the story that has been handed down from generation to generation. There is no doubt that it has been garnished in the telling. It may be a fairy tale, and the writer is inclined to think it is made out of whole cloth, but Mr. George Durnan, the late light keeper, states that he heard the story from his father, and that he, the son, with his uncle Joe Durnan, found in 1893, bits of a coffin and part of the jaw bone of a man four feet beneath the sand and about 500 feet west of the present keepers house. It was always claimed that Muller [*sic*] was buried west of the lighthouse, near the lagoon at the south end of Blockhouse Bay, and in order to verify the story, Mr. Durnan made the search with the above result."

It is likely that the spin about the mutilation and crude burial is nothing more than sensationalized fiction. O'Keeffe noted in one of his writings: "A close reading of Robertson's account provides the final nail in the coffin, so to speak, clearly implying that Durnan believed Radelmüller's corpse had been respectfully buried, not hacked to pieces and scattered. The discovery of coffin fragments found alongside a jawbone in 1893, if indeed linked to Radelmüller, would support such a conclusion but does not tally with a hasty burial by fugitive killers. Contrary to oft-repeated claims that the keeper was 'never seen again,' all evidence suggests that Radelmüller's body did not vanish in the first place but was found, examined by the coroner and laid to rest near the lighthouse."

Magdalena went on to acquire two hundred acres of land in Reach Township (York County in the Home District of Upper Canada) that was to be held in trust with her brother, Michael Burkholder, for her daughter. Arabella went on to marry a man named Adam Rupert and had several children before her death on September 19, 1844. She and Adam were buried at the Maple United Cemetery in Vaughan, Ontario—she as Ann Miller. Adam died forty years later on December 17, 1884. The date of Magdalena's death and her burial location are unknown.

Gibraltar Point Lighthouse, located on Centre Island in the Toronto Islands, was decommissioned in 1958, but the tower remains as a testament to the light's vast history. It is owned by the City of Toronto and can be reached via a ferry from May to October. The grey stone tower with its bright-red door sits in a park just over a mile from the ferry dock. Vehicles are prohibited on the island, but bike rentals are available. The light can also be viewed on sightseeing cruises of Toronto Harbour. Tours inside the tower are available on a limited basis by appointment only.

Toronto native Eamonn O'Keeffe, from whom the original interest in this story came, is completing his doctorate on British military musicians during the Napoleonic Wars and the Anglo-American War of 1812 at the University of Oxford. Aside from researching the Radelmüller case, he has published several academic articles and appeared as an expert on *Who Do You Think You Are?*, the BBC's hit family history show. O'Keeffe serves as a trustee for the Society for Army Historical Research and previously spent eleven years volunteering and working at Fort York, a War of 1812 historic site in Toronto.

PART II.

LAKE ERIE

2
SOUTH BASS ISLAND LIGHTHOUSE

PUT-IN-BAY, OHIO

Fear of contracting a devastating and severely contagious disease may have led to the suicide of a caretaker at the South Bass Island Lighthouse in Put-in-Bay, Ohio, in September 1898—the first of three untimely deaths within the light's history. And you know how they say things come in threes.

Lake Erie's 6,261,500 acres border four American states—New York, Pennsylvania, Ohio and Michigan—and the province of Ontario, Canada. Contained within this area of the Great Lakes are about thirty-six islands; some are large and developed, while others are small and uninhabited, according to LakeLubbers.com.

South Bass Island is part of the Bass Island Archipelago—a chain or cluster of islands within a specific body of water. It is the southernmost of the three Bass Islands (the others being, appropriately, Middle Bass Island and North Bass Island) and is noted as the third-largest island in Lake Erie. Other nearby islands in the archipelago include Ballast, Buckeye, Catawba, Gibraltar, Green, Kelley's, Lost Ballast, Mouse, Rattlesnake, Starve and Sugar Islands, all in Ohio, as well as East Sister, Hen (including her "chickens"—Big Chicken, Chick and Little Chicken), Middle, Middle Sister, North Harbor and Pelee Islands, all in Canadian waters.

The United States Lighthouse Service began planning the construction of the South Bass Island Lighthouse in 1893, selecting a site on the southernmost end of Parker Point to mark the Lake Erie passage from Sandusky to Toledo. A two-acre plot was eventually purchased, and after

A 1904 photograph of South Bass Island Lighthouse in Lake Erie, where three men (two keepers and an assistant) died. *Courtesy of the National Archives.*

some delay, the light was completed in 1897 for a cost of $8,600. The two-and-a-half-story brick Queen Anne–style house featured a three-story tower that was built into one corner to house an oil-fueled fourth-order Fresnel lens.

The first keeper there was a sailor named Harry H. Riley (sometimes printed as Henry, with variations on the middle initial, including K. and C.), who served eleven years (1886–97) aboard the lighthouse tender *Haze*.

According to the United States Lighthouse Society, the wooden tug *Haze* (once known as the *Dover*) was constructed in Mystic, Connecticut, in 1861 as a gunboat. It was rebuilt as a steam-powered propeller vessel in 1876 and was put into service as the first steam tender on the Great Lakes, replacing two sailing tenders operating in Lake Erie. The tender carried buoys and other supplies throughout Lake Erie and the Detroit River in the Great Lakes Tenth District until it was retired in 1905. Originally part of the U.S. Lighthouse Service (and now part of the coast guard), tenders were ships designed to serve, maintain, support and provide goods to lighthouses.

One would expect life on a tender to be physically demanding and, at times, dangerous in more ways than one, as was shared in the Tuesday,

May 19, 1891 issue of the *Buffalo Commercial* on page 11 under the headline "Assault on the High Seas—A Shooting Affair on the U.S. Supply Steamer 'Haze'":

> *Deputy U.S. Marshal Watts yesterday arrested John Carrera, first cook of the U.S. lighthouse supply steamer* Haze, *on a charge of assault with intent to kill, on the high seas, the complainant being the second engineer, Thomas Gilbert, who alleged that the cook fired a revolver at him on the afternoon of the 15th inst* [sic] *off Kelley's Island. The ball missed him, and no blood was shed.*
>
> *The case came on for examination at 11 o'clock today before U.S. commissioner Fitzgerald, and Wm. B. Hoyt appeared for the defendant, who is an undersized fellow and a native of Portugal. Engineer Gilbert testified that the defendant fired at him about 2 P.M. on the 15th, when the vessel was off Kelly's Island, and the ball lodged in the hatch combing. Gilbert admitted that he had been drinking freely and was pretty well under the influence of liquor at the time.*

Before becoming a lighthouse keeper, Harry H. Riley served aboard the lighthouse tender *Haze*, which serviced Lake Erie. *Courtesy of the U.S. Lighthouse Establishment.*

Captain John Baxter, of the Haze *testified that he hard* [sic] *the shot, went down, and took the revolver away from Carrera, and ordered him to go to the kitchen, which he did.*

First Mate Albert Hausten, Second Mate Harry H. Riley, Chief Engineer Charles E. Eckliff, and other members of the crew gave evidence, tending to show that Gilbert and the second cook had a quarrel first, then the first cook (the prisoner) appeared on the scene, and declaiming he would kill Gilbert, ran to his room and got his revolver, which he fired at Gilbert, the ball passing several inches above his head. All the witnesses thought Gilbert had been drinking.

Among the lighthouses in the Tenth District serviced by the *Haze* was the South Bass Island Lighthouse. So, it likely came as no surprise that Riley would make a natural progression of his career and move up the ranks from second mate of the tender to keeper at this newly constructed light.

An official letter from the Light-House Establishment, Office of the Light-House Inspector, Tenth District of Buffalo, New York, dated June 23, 1897, announced Riley's appointment as keeper.

Sirs:

I recommend the transfer, under the civil service regulations in regard to transfers, of Mr. Harry H. Riley, second mate of the tender Haze, *to the position of Keeper of the light station about to be established at South Bass Island, Lake Erie, (Ohio), the transfer to take effect July 10, 1897, and the salary of the keeper to be fixed at $560 annum.*

After a service of some three years as seaman (wheelman) in the Haze, *Mr. Riley was appointed second mate of that tender July 1, 1889, and discharged at the end of the season, December 15, 1889. He was reappointed second mate on March 10, 1890, since which date he has served continuously in that position.*

Mr. Riley also served one enlistment, three years, in the navy.

He is forty-one years of age, a native of the state of New York, a resident of Detroit, Michigan. He is perfectly familiar with the duties of a light-house keeper and entirely competent to perform them.

Respectfully yours, Theodor F. Jewell Commander, U.S.N., Inspector 10th L.H. District.

On August 8, 1898—a little more than a year after moving into the lighthouse with his wife—Riley hired an eccentric Black man named Samuel Anderson as a part-time caretaker to assist in the daily duties at the lighthouse. This arrangement included room and board in the basement of the lighthouse. Anderson was regarded as a dedicated worker, a bit of a loner and a collector of live snakes.

In addition to his service at the lighthouse, Anderson was said to have worked at the nearby Hotel Victory. The cornerstone for this massive Queen Anne–style building was laid on September 10, 1889, and when it opened on July 29, 1892, it was noted as one of the largest hotels in America at the time and one of the most expensive, with a million-dollar price tag ($29.2 million today). Set on a one-hundred-acre parcel, the hotel featured 625 guest rooms (80 with private baths); 2 dining rooms that sat a collective 1,200 guests simultaneously; a 700-seat auditorium; 3 elevators; a wine cellar, livery, greenhouse, barbershop, tailor, manicurist, ice cream parlor, billiard room, newsstand, photography darkroom and in-house dentist; and private parlors, shops and servants' quarters. There was even a dedicated trolley line to transport guests between the resort and town, where the ferry docks remain today.

But the grand Hotel Victory was soon facing defeat. Less than two months after opening, it fell into receivership, and the following year's 1893 stock market crash dealt another rough blow that led to the hotel's temporary closure on August 5 of that year. In 1895, the original architect (and the only bidder) scooped up the building for a mere $17,000—minus the furnishings, which were acquired by another creditor for $7,000.

On July 20, 1896 (nearly four years after the hotel's original opening), the Hotel Victory was once again welcoming guests. Two years later, a thirty-

The Victory Hotel welcomed guests for only twenty-five years before the largest fire the Erie island had ever seen tore through the structure on August 14, 1919. It was a total loss, and today, all that remains are ruins, located inside the South Bass Island State Park. *Author's collection.*

by-one-hundred-foot natatorium (swimming pool) was added to the hotel's amenities, and some say it was the first that allowed both men and women to congregate together.

But 1898 turned out to be another difficult year for the hotel, and in fact, it was challenging for the island and the state of Ohio. From Cleveland to Put-in-Bay, a smallpox epidemic broke out, and South Bass Island was placed under quarantine.

According to the World Health Organization, "smallpox is an acute contagious disease caused by the variola virus, a member of the orthopoxvirus family. It was one of the world's most devastating diseases known to humanity." In a seven-year period, from 1898 to 1904, Ohio tallied up the cases and casualties; on average, 3 out of every 10 people who caught the virus died. Those who lived were often left with scars or even deformities. While early vaccines were developed, they weren't always readily available, and in some cases, they were deadly themselves. The peak epidemic year in Ohio was 1902, with over 1,200 cases and nearly 225 deaths.

During the epidemic's first year, twenty-six employees from the Hotel Victory were infected (while Cleveland on the mainland reported seventy cases). Despite the low contraction levels in 1898, Sam Anderson became increasingly paranoid that he would fall victim to the virus. Just three weeks into his lighthouse employment, he set out to leave the area for safer pastures, but before he could get very far the lockdown was in place. No one was allowed to come onto South Bass Island, and certainly, no one was allowed to leave.

Julie Majo, an Ohio genealogist and historian who has been researching the keepers of South Bass Island Lighthouse, shared her thoughts about Sam and his service under Harry Riley. In an email dated July 17, 2020, she stated:

> *When smallpox was identified, Sam Anderson was among those quarantined, confined to the lighthouse station on South Bass Island. He attempted to escape but was sent back on August 30, 1898. He refused to enter the lighthouse, insisting that if he remained at the station, he would surely die. This statement was attributed to an obsessive fear of smallpox. This seems implausible. He was safe from contagion at the lighthouse but at risk of infection in quarantine with his friends. He was afraid of something worse at the lighthouse. By this time, Harry was exhibiting increasingly bizarre behavior and thoughts* [the cause of which is revealed later in this chapter]. *It's hard to say whether he had quarreled with Sam or*

In den Tod getrieben

hat die Furcht vor den Blattern den
Neger Sam Anderson auf Put-in-
Bay. Er suchte seine Furcht im
Trunk zu ersäufen und flüchtete sich in
seinem Rausche in den Keller des
Leuchtthurms, nicht weit von dem Hotel Victory, wo er Anfälle von Säu-
ferwahnsinn hatte. Am Dienstag
Nacht kam er heraus, ging hinunter
an die Werfte und mit dem Schrei:
„God save them all," sprang er in
den See und ertrank. Seine Leiche
wurde am Mittwoch aufgefischt.

"Driven to death...by the fear of the pox was the negro Sam Anderson on Put-in-Bay. He tried to drown his fear in alcohol—and in his intoxication, he fled into the basement of the lighthouse, not far from the Hotel Victory, where he suffered bouts of booze madness. On Tuesday night, he came down to the shipyard, and with the scream 'God save them all,' he jumped into the lake—and drowned. His body was found on Wednesday." *From the* Fremont Courier, *September 8, 1898.*

threatened him, but it is interesting to note that [Sam] *refused to go in the basement where the collection of snakes was kept. Most people would see to the welfare of their pets.*

It appears that no one took the trouble to ask questions about his fear, or if they did, they dismissed their answers. After his death, there was reason to minimize his concerns and the poor judgement that resulted in his death. It is said that he howled and screamed for help all night long. This may be an exaggeration. It is not reported who was witness to his distress.

On the morning of August 31, 1898, his body was found on the rocks of the cliff near the lighthouse. The case was quickly labeled a suicide. It is hard to say whether he was killed by Harry or fell fleeing him. It seems unlikely that a man who begged for his life all night committed suicide. It was unthinkable that he would be expected to provide posthumous justice for a Black man at the risk of the reputation of a White government official. At any rate, investigation of his death seemed to be minimal, and his Black friends were sent away soon after.

After his death, Sam was described as peculiar, eccentric, a drunkard and a keeper of snakes. This seems implausible, since he had been hired only a few weeks earlier and, at the time, was deemed a qualified candidate. No talk of his odd ways was reported prior to his death. He was welcomed into the society of other Black residents.

Files obtained through the University Libraries Archives at Ohio State University (OSU) in Columbus included a statement about Sam's death that was released nearly two months later, on October 21, 1898, from the Tenth

District of the Light-House Establishment of Buffalo, New York, to the Light-House Board in Washington, D.C. "Samuel Anderson worked at the South Bass Island Lt. Sta. O., 17½ days from Aug. 9 to Aug. 30, '98, inclusive, at a rate of $1.00 per day, giving a total credit of $17.25 for his services. Subsequently, and before he was paid the sum due him, he committed suicide. I inclose [*sic*] herewith a letter dated Oct. 6, '98 from Wm. H. King, justice of the peace and coroner of Put-in-Bay, South Bass Island, stating that no relative appeared to defray the burial and inquest expenses and that he assumes the authority as an officer of the law to all monies and property found in his [Samuel Anderson's] possession at the time of his death or due to him, to defray his funeral expenses. I have the honor to request if there is any authority of law regulation by which I can pay Mr. King $17.25, the amount due Samuel Anderson at his death as above stated, to be applied in payment of published expenses incurred on account of inquest and funeral. Respectfully yours, T.W. Symons, Major of Engineers, U.S.A., Engineer 10th L.H. District."

The "Record of Deaths" for the Ottawa County Probate Court in 1898 noted Anderson's death as suicide. While some accounts state that he was an "elderly" man, the age printed on his death record was just thirty-eight. According to local historians, he was buried in the pauper's field in South Bass Island's Crown Hill Cemetery, located inside the front gate under what is now a gravel driveway. No record of his burial or headstone can be found.

But the tragic history of the South Bass Island Lighthouse didn't end there. Just days after Anderson's death, on September 1, Harry Riley seemed to become delusional. He was found on the mainland, wandering aimlessly near the city of Sandusky (some twenty-four miles away). He was incoherent, and some even speculated he was under the influence of something. "Harry was heard telling all who would listen that he had the fastest horse in the area," according to HauntedToledo.com. "He would approach total strangers and invite them to the fairgrounds just so they could see how fast it would go and claimed it was fast enough to break any speed record." But interestingly enough, Riley didn't own any horses.

On September 2, 1898, the *Sandusky Star* reported on the incident under the headline: "LIGHTHOUSE KEEPER DEMENTED. Harry Riley of Put-in-Bay Thought He Owned a Race Horse":

"Harry H. Riley, the lighthouse keeper at Put-in-Bay, was arrested last evening and locked up for safekeeping. Riley was demented and had the idea that he owned a fast horse. He was buying a harness and other trappings and invited everybody to go out to the fairgrounds today to see the horse go for a record.

"Mayor Zimmerman received a telegram this morning from Riley's wife, asking that he be detained until she could come after him. This will be done.

"Considerable excitement was caused after Riley's arrest by the report that he was an escaped small-pox patient. There was no truth in this rumor, but people were much afraid of him."

An update was published the following day in the same paper under the headline "Harry Riley Insane":

"Harry H. Riley, the demented lighthouse keeper at Put-in-Bay, will be taken before Probate Judge Goodwin this afternoon for a hearing as to his sanity. Mrs. Riley arrived today from Put-in-Bay, but her husband is in such a condition that he cannot be taken home. It was thought best to send him to an asylum where he can receive proper treatment."

Still newsworthy on September 6, the news came that Riley had been taken to Port Clinton in nearby Ottawa County. "Sheriff [Sigmund] Leimgruber of Ottawa county, took Harry H. Riley, the demented lighthouse keeper of Put-in-Bay, to Port Clinton yesterday. An inquest as to his sanity will be held in the probate court of that county."

A copy of the official inquest document, found in the OSU Archives, was dated September 7, 1898, and two days later, a letter from the Tenth District commander Franklin Hanford was sent to the Light-House Service in Washington, D.C., that read: "By letter dated September 3^{d}, 1898, the keeper of Green Island Light-Station reported that on the day previous Mr. Harry H. Riley, keeper South Bass Island Light-Station, Lake Erie, Ohio, was arrested as an insane person at Sandusky, Ohio, and would be sent to the asylum for the insane at Toledo, Ohio, and that under orders from the collector of customs at Sandusky, Ohio, he had sent Mr. Otto to take charge of the light.

"I have authorized Mrs. Riley, the wife of the keeper, to take charge of the station as laborer-in-charge on receipt of my letter. Supposing then to terminate the services of Mr. Richey and to retain Mrs. Riley in charge for a short time until the probable result of her husband's illness shall be determined."

On September 10, 1898—a week after his arrest—Riley was admitted to the Toledo State Hospital (also known as the Northern Ohio Lunatic Asylum) for observation. Opened in 1888, this facility was built in a modern gothic revival style and was the first institution designed to the "cottage plan system." According to AsylumProjects.com: "The cottage plan (also known as the colony plan in England) is a style of asylum planning that gained popularity at the very end of the 19th century and continued to be very

On September 10, 1898, Harry H. Riley, keeper of the South Bass Island Lighthouse, was admitted to the Toledo State Hospital (also known as the Northern Ohio Lunatic Asylum) for observation. *From AsylumProjects.com.*

popular well into the 20th century. Early cottage plan buildings were typically no more than two stories tall; they were typically built of fireproof materials, such as brick, stone, and slate. They were purposely built for a single type of patient, and there were typically two sets of buildings for each, one for women and one for men. Hospital campuses usually resembled that of a college with large, well-manicured lawns, flower beds, trees, fountains, and other decorative items."

Riley was diagnosed as clinically insane and was housed in the men's ward, where he received treatment for his condition. He was officially removed from his lighthouse service duties on February 23, 1899, and official records from Lighthouse Inspector Franklin Hanford noted that the keeper was "hopelessly insane."

Early speculation, especially around South Bass Island, was that Riley had been driven mad by what had happened to Anderson that fateful day near the lighthouse—perhaps out of guilt for causing his death in some way.

Julie Majo, who also contributes to the Toledo State Hospital Cemeteries' Facebook page, shared the actual details of Harry's crazy behavior as part of a follow-up email on July 17, 2020.

> *Harry Riley suffered and died from paretic dementia. He did not "suddenly" become insane. Another term for paretic dementia is "general paralysis of the insane." The modern term is advanced neurosyphilis. It is a severe neuropsychiatric disorder caused by late-stage syphilis* [the affliction that ultimately killed Chicago gangster Al Capone in 1947]. *It leads to cerebral atrophy, among other things. Untreated syphilis is a horrible disease, and before penicillin, it was the primary diagnosis for 25% of patients in government mental hospitals. GPI generally appeared 10–30 years after initial infection, and death generally occurred within five years of the first symptoms. As the disease progresses, mental deterioration occurs. Typical symptoms included loss of social inhibitions; asocial behavior; gradual impairment of judgement, concentration and short-term memory; euphoria; mania; depression; or apathy. Delusions are common. Eventually, the patient dies, bedridden, emaciated, completely disoriented and often suffering from continual seizures.*
>
> *The early symptoms may have been the reason Harry was transferred from active duty on the tender* Haze *to take the less-challenging and lower-paid position of lighthouse keeper. Within a year, Harry was having trouble carrying out the duties of maintaining the lighthouse and grounds and hired a caretaker: Sam Anderson.*
>
> *When Harry was arrested in Sandusky, it was determined that he had gone insane. This was a natural progress of his disorder. His wife was not surprised and knew his condition was more than she could handle. She promoted the idea of a transfer to a mental hospital. She returned to the lighthouse to continue her duties as de facto lighthouse keeper* [until Enoch W. Scribner took over].

While there is no way to know when Riley contracted the disease or, therefore, how long he suffered with it, we know it eventually consumed him. He died at the asylum on March 11, 1899, at the age of just forty-two, just six months and one day after he was institutionalized.

Riley's death record notes that his body was sent to Holland, New York (Erie County), for interment. One source indicated that he was buried in the Old Holland Cemetery (formerly called the Holland Protestant Cemetery), the second-oldest cemetery in town. However, an exhaustive online search of cemetery records for that cemetery and all Erie County cemeteries, as well as graveyards in neighboring counties, have yielded zero results. One could assume Riley was sent to this small western New York town because of his family ties or the fact that he was born or raised there, but in reviewing census data, no connections were found between him and other Rileys in the area.

Attempts to find Riley's body in Toledo also fell flat, despite the fact that for nearly a century, from 1888 to 1973, the bodies of those who died at the asylum and weren't claimed by family were buried in one of two on-site cemeteries. During that time, nearly two thousand people were buried beneath small concrete blocks marked only with a burial number.

Charles B. Duggan was the keeper of the South Bass Island Lighthouse for seventeen years, from 1911 to 1925, until he died tragically there. *Courtesy of the Kraig Anderson and LighthouseFriends.com.*

In 2005, the Toledo State Hospital Cemetery Reclamation Project was established in cooperation with the University of Toledo (the owner of the properties that contain the cemeteries) and Northwest Ohio Psychiatric Hospital (the current facility was constructed after the original asylum closed in 1982 and subsequently razed) to restore the two patient cemeteries. "Even these anonymous grave markers were eventually lost underground after decades of neglect. The city grew up around the cemeteries, and the people buried there were forgotten," according to ToledoStateHospitalCemetery.org. "Grave markers are being located and raised above ground, monuments and a bench have been installed followed by a footpath in the near future, and families are finding their lost ancestors."

Given Mrs. Riley's first name was never known, her history after Harry's death—including her internment location—remains a mystery.

More than two decades passed at the South Bass Island Lighthouse before its next tragedy was recorded—yet another keeper met his death along the rocky shoreline.

Charles B. Duggan was born March 14, 1866, in Sacketts Harbor, New York, to Richard and Roxanne (Case) Duggan. He began his lighthouse service in 1903 as the principal keeper of the West Sister Island Lighthouse in Lake Erie before being transferred to South Bass Island in 1908. Charles lived at the lighthouse with his wife, Bertha (Graham), and their three sons: Arthur, Archie and Lyle.

In addition to his keeper duties, Duggan was a farmer with a valuable tract of twenty acres, including peach orchards and eight acres for wine grapes. He was also involved in various civic and community organizations, including the Democratic Party, Freemasons, Independent Order of Odd Fellows at Sacketts Harbor, New York, and the Foresters in Sandusky, Ohio.

Duggan is noted as the longest-serving keeper at the South Bass Island Lighthouse, putting in seventeen years before he fell to his death on April 29, 1925, at the age of fifty-nine. His official certificate of death reads: "accidental—fell over 30-foot cliff on west end South Bass Island." The story was told in an article under the headline "Captain Duggan Falls to Death at Put-in Bay":

> *Apparently losing his footing in the darkness or because the ledge on which he was walking gave way, Captain Charles H.* [sic] *Duggan, 59, keeper of the South Bass Island light, fell 30 feet to his death here last night while on his way to the lighthouse from the home of O.L. Miller.*
>
> *When Captain Duggan failed to return home Wednesday night, his son started a search for him and the body, with gashes on the head and temples, was found this morning about midway between Stone Cove and the light.*
>
> *Duggan left the Miller home at 7:50 last night, and refusing a lift started to walk home, his path leading along the edge of a cliff. At the spot where the body was found,* [the] *descent of the cliff was impossible, and it was necessary to take boats from the harbor, two miles away, in order to recover the remains. Death was pronounced accidental at a coroner's examination, and Ed Quick Sandusky, undertaker, took charge of the funeral arrangements.*
>
> *Duggan was born at Sackett's Harbor,* [New York,] *and entered the life-saving service at Buffalo in 1898 and in 1903 went to West Sister Island as a light keeper. In 1908, he was moved to Put-in-Bay.*
>
> *He is survived by his widow, formerly Miss Bertha Graham, to whom he was married on May 8, 1892, and three sons, Arthur, of Cleveland, Archie, of Los Angeles, Calif., and Lyle, of this place.*

Duggan was buried on May 2 in the Maple Leaf Cemetery in Put-in-Bay. His headstone was the only one from these three keepers to be found. Immediately following his death, Bertha and, later, his son Lyle took over temporary lighthouse duties until William L. Gordon arrived in December.

The South Bass Island Lighthouse operated until 1962, and five years later, it was purchased by Ohio State University (OSU) to serve as a research facility. It is believed to be the only lighthouse in the United States currently owned by a university.

Listed in the National Register of Historic Places on April 5, 1990, South Bass Island Lighthouse is open for tours on select dates during the summer season and by arrangement for groups of ten or more. It is one of only five island sites recognized by the Ohio Historic Preservation Office for its architectural or historical significance (others include the Foster-Gram House, Green Island Lighthouse, Inselruhe Mansion, Perry's Victory and International Peace Memorial). Not on the list is the Hotel Victory, which was destroyed by fire on August 14, 1919. Today, its ruins can be viewed on the grounds of the South Bass Island State Park.

South Bass Island is accessible by Miller Ferry and Jet Express, which offer seasonal service from Port Clinton, Catawaba Island, Sandusky and Marblehead, home of the oldest continuously operating lighthouse on the American side of the Great Lakes, dating back to the early 1820s (see the last chapter for more). Ferries generally run between May and October.

PART III.

LAKE HURON

3

CLAPPERTON ISLAND LIGHTHOUSE

MANITOULIN ISLANDS, CANADA

The Baker family had longstanding ties to Clapperton Island Lighthouse, located just north of Kagawong in the north channel of Georgian Bay in Ontario, Canada. In all, the men in this family served continually from 1875 to 1962.

Benjamin Booth Baker was the patriarch of this family, born on December 3, 1820, in Kingston, Ontario. He had one child with his first wife, Ajaine "Jane" (Quinbury), and six children—including Henry Frederick (born on September 22, 1864, in Caledonia, Ontario)—with his second wife, a widow and mother of six named Isabella Munce (also spelled Muntz or Muntzed). Henry later married Jennie Anne "Jane" (Gordon), and they had six children of their own, including William Benjamin (born on April 22, 1897, in Gore Bay, Ontario) and James Frederick "Earl" (born on June 21, 1906). These four Baker men all served their own stints at the Clapperton Island Lighthouse, and each had their own interesting story to tell.

According to LighthouseFriends.com: "The North Channel has a length of roughly 160 nautical miles and connects Georgian Bay on the east to St. Marys River on the west. The channel is bordered by the mainland on the north, and on the south by the islands of Manitoulin, Cockburn, Drummond, and St. Joseph, and is connected to Lake Huron by Mississagi Strait between Manitoulin Island and Cockburn Island and False Detour Channel between Cockburn Island and Drummond Island. The North Channel is recognized as one of the best freshwater cruising grounds in the world."

The lighthouse on Clapperton Island was built in 1866. During its nearly one-hundred-year history, there were only five head keepers, and three of them were members of the Baker family. *From Norman Lloyd, as printed in* The North Channel and St. Mary's River.

The lighthouse on Clapperton Island was built in 1866. During its nearly one-hundred-year history (ninety-eight to be exact, until 1964), there were only five head keepers, and three of them were Bakers (one Baker also served as an assistant). A posting on the Manitoulin History Facebook group made by Marie Leeney noted: "Like all lighthouse families, the Bakers did many jobs to supplement their modest pay for keeping the light. They maintained the channel buoys, guided fishermen and sold their catch to the crew of the SS *Normac* when it delivered coal oil for the lamps. In the winter, they trapped and cut timber. They raised cattle, sheep and grew vegetables on their own farm at the centre of the island, and lived in their farmhouse all winter."

Benjamin Baker was only the second keeper of the Clapperton Island Lighthouse, serving from 1875 until he disappeared nineteen years later. Historian and author Fred Stonehouse told the story in his book *Great Lakes Crime: Murder, Mayhem, Booze & Broads* (2004, 3–4):

> *All went along fine until one day in September 1894, when Bejamin's son, Henry, noticed his father's small sailboat drifting past the island. It looked empty of life except for his loyal dog. Alarmed, Henry quickly launched another rowboat and went out to investigate. Benjamin had earlier gone ashore to the small community of Gore Bay for an evening of card playing and an occasional snort of good drink'n whiskey. Going to Gore Bay was a*

> *common activity for Benjamin. What could have happened to him? When he reached the sailboat, Henry discovered a partially filled whisky bottle rolling around on the floor and his father's empty wallet. Since there wasn't a bank anywhere close, it was common for Benjamin to carry a pretty hefty wad of cash with him. What happened to it? He certainly wouldn't have gambled it all away! And more important, where was his father? Did he fall out of the boat and drown? If so, why was the wallet still aboard? He would have carried it in his pocket and not left it lying on the thwart. In spite of the obvious questions, the Canadian authorities never pursued the mystery.*

To this day, the death of Benjamin remains a mystery—was it an accident or murder? Since his body was never found, there is no grave marker for him. Isabelle lived to be eighty-five years old, passing away on March 25, 1912. She was buried in Oakland Cemetery in Glencoe (Middlesex County), Ontario. At the time of her death, she had nearly one hundred grandchildren and great-grandchildren.

Henry stepped into the head position at Clapperton Island Lighthouse after his father's disappearance, serving for forty-five years (until 1939). One of the most interesting things that happened during Henry's tenure occurred in July 1924, based on a newspaper article published in the *Ottawa Journal* under the headline "FLOATING BODY REVEALS MURDER NORTH COUNTRY":

"Provincial police here are endeavoring to ascertain the identity of the headless body of a man discovered floating in the water off Bedford Island, near here, by lumberjacks over the weekend. Finding of the mutilated corpse brings to light evidence of a brutal murder presumably committed some weeks ago.

"The body had been bound, hand and foot, with clothesline, but this had rotted through. It had been attached to a heavy weight, and when the line broke, the body was released and came to the surface. Gulls circling about above the corpse attracted the attention of workers in a nearby lumber camp, and they investigated.

"Constable Shields is in charge of the case. The body was badly decomposed, and so far, efforts to identify the remains have been to no avail. From the state of the body, it is believed the murder was committed with an axe, the head being completely severed."

According to Stonehouse, the still-unidentified Native in question was working for Henry when he disappeared in November 1923, although one newspaper account said the man worked in a local lumber camp. It was Henry, however, who identified what was left of the man's body. This led to the subsequent investigation of his death.

A week later, the identity of the headless man made the news in the July 11, 1924 issue of the *Windsor Star* under the revealing headline "MOTHER, SON HELD IN DEATH OF MAN":

> *The body of the man found in the waters of the north channel near Bedford Island, about eight miles from Little Current, Manitoulin Island, on July 1, and which was reported only a few days ago, has been identified as that of Angus Corbierre, an Indian.*
>
> *Authorities still adhere to the belief that he was murdered, and following disclosures at the inquest held by Coroner Major, the victim's wife and her grown-up son have been taken into custody and lodged in the district jail.*
>
> *Dr. Young examined the body and expressed the opinion that the man had been dead and decapitated before the body was put in the water. When found, the body was anchored by a common wire clothesline, which was bound about his legs. The boots were identified by one witness as a pair worn by an Indian named Angus Corbierre of West Bay."*

The following day, the *Gazette* out of Montreal added further details about "Big Angus," as the man was known. "The Indian had been missing since the first week in November last. He had been working in a lumber camp on Clapperton Island, where he had been living for some time with his wife, a widow whom he married about two years ago. About the time of his disappearance, his wife returned to the reserve at West Bay and said that her husband had gone on a long hunting trip, and her son, who brought her home, said a short time ago that Angus had gone to Minnesota and that he had been seen there by a cousin. The wire clothesline found on the body was identified by one witness as the same as some he had seen at the camp of the Corbierres at Clapperton Island. The inquest was adjourned, and the testimony of other witnesses will be taken."

No further articles were found that gave details about a trial of the wife and her son or of where Corbierre's body was finally laid to rest.

Years later, at the age of eighty-two, Henry was involved in an accident that ultimately resulted in his alarming death. On his burial listing on FindAGrave.com, it is noted: "Mr. Baker, who retired as lighthouse keeper some years ago, was in the habit of assisting his son, Wm. Baker, who is the present keeper, with the range lights. Friday [September 17, 1946], as usual, he rode on horseback to the range light and hoisted it. After the light reached the top, the rope broke, and it came crashing down, hitting Baker on the shoulder. The injured man managed to get on his horse and rode the 1½ mile back to the house. Saturday morning, he was taken to the hospital [St. Joseph] here, where he passed on Tuesday morning."

Henry was buried in the Gordon Cemetery in Gordon, Ontario.

William Baker was the third Baker (in three generations) to take the helm at Clapperton Island Lighthouse, from 1940 to 1962, with his brother, Earl, working as an assistant keeper at least at the time of his accidental death on Sunday, October 26, 1947. One news brief in the *Windsor Star* that was printed a few days later said that Earl had been hunting with Grant Rogers, proprietor of the Harbour Island Tourist Camp, when the two became separated at dusk. Rogers apparently mistook Earl Baker for a deer, firing a shot that hit the assistant keeper in the head. He was taken to the Little Current Hospital, where he died the same day. Earl was buried at the Gordon Cemetery in Ontario, along with other members of the family.

As the final keeper in the family to serve, William took his job seriously—very seriously. In fact, even when afflicted by a debilitating appendicitis in September 1950, he refused to leave his post. For three days, the fifty-six-year-old keeper endured the excruciating pain, yet he was found collapsed on the path to the lighthouse, where he was trying to crawl the thirty to forty yards to the light to refill the oil in the lamps.

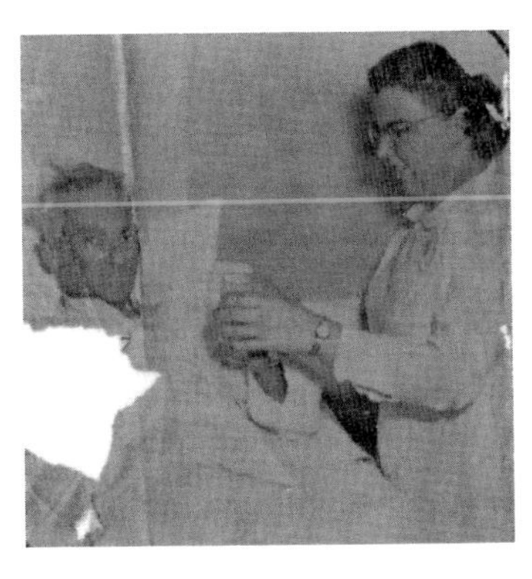

William Baker was so dedicated to his job as a lighthouse keeper that even when he was afflicted by a debilitating appendicitis, he refused to leave his post. He was later found collapsed outside the building, as he was trying to crawl the thirty or forty yards to the light to refill the oil in the lamps. He was subsequently hospitalized. *From the* Ottawa Journal.

"Five hours later, Harold Hutchings, who lives four miles away on Harbour Island, rowed to the lighthouse with Bert Bailey of Kagawong to return some articles he had borrowed from Baker. He found Baker lying semidelirious and bathed in sweat," said a September 19 article in the *Ottawa Journal*.

"'I'm done, boys,' Baker whispered to Hutchins and Bailey. 'Get Norm Lloyd [Baker's nephew] from Kagawong to look after the light. It's out of oil.'

"Hutchings and Bailey half carried, half dragged the sick man to their boat and brought him to Kagawong, on the northern shore of Manitoulin Island. Then they took him by automobile eighteen miles to the Red Cross hospital at Mindemoya.

"Doctors performed an emergency operation to remove a ruptured appendix. They said today that Baker's condition is satisfactory and that he should soon be in good shape to go back to his lighthouse."

After his surgery, William did return to his lighthouse and served as keeper until he retired in 1962. While visiting his sister, Mrs. Marshall Brown, in Wayne, Michigan, William passed away on March 24, 1969 (a month before his seventy-second birthday). It is said he had been battling a lengthy illness. He was interred in the Gorden Cemetery in Ontario, along with his father, Henry, and brother, Earl.

After William's retirement, Glenn McFarlene was appointed the final keeper of the Clapperton Island Lighthouse, serving just two years until it was automated.

Clapperton Island is only accessible by chartering a private boat from Gore Bay, although nothing remains of the lighthouse or the keeper's residence.

The nearby Benjamin Islands, a small group of islands that lie toward the eastern end of the North Channel, were named for Benjamin Baker. They are regarded as some of the most beautiful islands in this region. The harbor is formed by the two main islands: North and South Benjamin Islands. A listing on Great-Lakes-Sailing.com notes that, "Sculpted and carved by glaciers, wind and weather, these pink granite islands offer breathtaking views; still, quiet nights; star-studded skies; and the shimmering northern lights."

PART IV.

LAKE MICHIGAN

4
ST. HELENA ISLAND LIGHTHOUSE (AND OTHER STRAITS OF MACKINAC LIGHTS)

The Marshalls were among a handful of families who made lighthouse keeping a "business" in the Straits of Mackinac area. Between 1870 and 1966, at least twelve men (and three generations) served at various lights in this region, with over 310 combined years of service. Two of these men lost their lives in the line of duty when they drowned. Another suffered for years from an on-the-job injury he received at St. Helena Island Lighthouse before he finally succumbed.

The patriarch of this large and impressive family was William David Marshall, who was born in 1800 in New York. Although he never served as a lighthouse keeper himself, his years of military service clearly inspired his male descendants to follow in his governmental footsteps. William D. and his wife, Fanny Anne (Hawkins), had ten children—five sons (and a son-in-law) went into lighthouse service. Known as the "Old Sergeant," William D. served in the military for sixty-two years, and according to his obituary, "[he] was, without a doubt, the oldest enlisted man in the army of the United States" when he died at the age of eighty-three in 1884. In fact, he was still an enlisted man at the time of his passing.

In 1834, the first son born to William D. and Fanny (and the first in the line to tend a Michigan lighthouse) was William Anthony. Between 1890 and 1907, William A. served at four Straits-area lights: Skillagalee (Ile Aux Galets, meaning "Isle of Pebbles" in French), Spectacle Reef Lighthouse, Bois Blanc Island Lighthouse and Round Island Lighthouse.

James C. Marshall was an assistant keeper at Spectacle Reef Lighthouse in Lake Huron (working with his father, William A.) when he drowned in April 1883 at the age of twenty-one. His body was never recovered, but there is a marker dedicated to him at St. Ann's Catholic Cemetery on Mackinac Island. *Courtesy of Mike Cronk.*

William A. married Matilda (or Mathilda) LaDuke (or Ladue), and their son, James C., began his keeper career working alongside his father at the Spectacle Reef Lighthouse in 1882, but he died at the age of twenty-one the following year. In April 1883, father and son were on a boat, traveling between their lighthouse and nearby Mackinac Island, when a sudden gust of wind overturned the small boat and threw James into the frigid waters, where he subsequently drowned. His body was never recovered, but there is a marker dedicated to him at St. Ann's Catholic Cemetery on Mackinac Island.

Thomas was born in 1837, the second son of William D. and Fanny. He served in the military for one year during the Civil War before he was shot in the shoulder, discharged and sent back to Michigan, where he eventually joined the growing family business. He landed at Spectacle Reef in 1879, working alongside his older brother, William A. In 1882, he was promoted and transferred to the nearby Waugoshance Shoal Lighthouse (southwest of Mackinaw City), serving as principal keeper until his death on May 28, 1886, at the age of forty-eight. Like his nephew a few years prior, Thomas drowned while returning from Mackinac Island. There is no information on whether his body was ever recovered, but a tombstone with his name can be found in the Protestant Cemetery on Mackinac Island, alongside that of another brother, Samuel, who died in 1881 at the age of twenty-eight. Thomas's parents and several of his brothers were also buried nearby.

Other keeper sons of William D. and Fanny included:

- George Washington, born in 1845, was a Civil War soldier with engagements in the Battles of Gettysburg, Wilderness and Appomattox. He served at Waugoshance, working for his brother Thomas until Thomas died. At that time, George was transferred to serve as the first keeper at the Mackinac Point Lighthouse when it was put into operation in 1890. He served there for twenty-nine years before retiring in 1919, turning the job over to his adoptive son, James Merritt (who later tended the Muskegon South Pierhead Light, Waugoshance Shoal and White Shoal until a stroke forced his retirement in 1941).

- Walter Green, born in 1849, ran away to become a sailor on the Great Lakes at the age of sixteen, and after seven years, he entered the lighthouse service. His first years were served aboard a tender, but he was eventually hired at Spectacle Reef Lighthouse, where he put in an impressive thirty-six years. He also served as head keeper of the DeTour Reef Lighthouse, near the current ferry to Drummond Island. He ended his service at the Windmill Point Lighthouse on the shores of Lake St. Claire in what is now Grosse Pointe Park in southeast Michigan before retiring in 1919. He and his wife, Mary Agetha (Louisignau), had ten or eleven children—including three sons (following) who were noted lighthouse keepers.

  - Francis or "Frank," born in 1877, was the first-born son to Walter and Mary and served at Stannard Rock Lighthouse, Keweenaw Waterway (Portage River) Upper Entrance Light and Devil's Island Lighthouse in the Apostle Islands and finally at the Port Austin Reef Light at the tip of Michigan's thumb region, where he retired in 1942.

  - Arthur S., born in 1879, worked at the Manitou Island Lighthouse near Copper Harbor and the Keweenaw Peninsula, the Spectacle Reef Lighthouse and finally the Detroit River/Bar Point Shoal Light before retiring and switching careers in 1912.

  - Joseph "Joe" B., born in 1890, was a private in Company K, Third Regiment Michigan Volunteer Infantry out of Cheboygan, and it appears he served in World War I. He was a lighthouse keeper at Rock of Ages, Point Iroquois and Superior Entry/Wisconsin Point Lighthouse, all in Lake Superior. He served twenty years in total, from 1927 to 1947.

- William Barnum, a son-in-law, was married to Sarah Marshall (born in 1861), the youngest daughter of William D. and Fanny. Barnum began his lighthouse career in 1902 as a laborer at Waugoshance Shoal Lighthouse. He then served two years at the Seul Choix Point Light in Gulliver, followed by tenures at Skillagalee, St. Helena Island, Mackinac Point and White Shoal, before retiring in 1929 after twenty-seven combined years of service.

The most interesting and tragic Marshall family story belongs to Charles, the youngest son of William D. and Fanny, who was born on March 18, 1858. After my visit to St. Helena Island in the Straits of Mackinac in the summer of 2019, it was his story that prompted the deep dive into the Marshall family lighthouse history. As shocking as some of the previous stories have been, it is Charles's narrative that is truly unfortunate, considering the length of time in which he suffered.

As late as the 1880 census, a twenty-one-year-old Charles was still living with his parents on Mackinac Island with a noted occupation as a laborer. In 1884, Charles began his eighteen-year lighthouse career as a second assistant at Waugoshance Shoal Lighthouse (which had been built in 1851 for a whopping $83,945, nearly $3 million today). His bosses at that time were none other than his brothers, Thomas (who was head keeper) and George W. (who was first assistant). The Marshall family had total control over this unique offshore light station for two years. When Thomas died in 1886 after his boat capsized in the Straits of Mackinac, George W. moved up to the head position, and Charles was promoted to first assistant.

Twelve miles across the water, St. Helena Island had served as a workshop or warehouse of sorts during the construction of Waugoshance. According to LighthouseFriends.com, "when work began on Waugoshance Lighthouse in 1847, St. Helena was used as a base of operations where wooden piers were constructed before being towed out toward the shoal and filled with stone."

Twenty-five years later, St. Helena Island was preparing for its own lighthouse, which was completed and put into operation in 1873. The 240-acre island had supported active fishing and shipping businesses operated

The St. Helena Island Lighthouse was completed and put into operation in the western Straits of Mackinac in northern Lake Michigan in 1873. *Courtesy of the National Archives.*

by Archie and Wilson Newton as early as the 1850s, although they likely expected their community of about two hundred people to thrive for more than just thirty years.

Sometime in the late 1880s, Charles married Rose Costello (or Costella, as noted on some records), who was born around 1870 in Ireland. The couple had six children—five girls and one boy.

In July 1888, a thirty-year-old Charles accepted a promotion and raise in pay (from $410 to $560 a year) to serve as the principal keeper of the St. Helena Island Lighthouse. Island life suited him and Rose well, and they soon began building their family. Olive was born in September 1891, followed by Jessie in January 1893; Ethel on October 4, 1894; Hazel on November 23, 1897; Nora (or Norah) May on December 22, 1899; and Chester Bernard on February 18, 1900 (the last year the family resided at their island lighthouse).

The agonizing story of the end of Charles's twelve-year tenure on St. Helena Island was described in detail on LighthouseFriends.com:

All alone on the island, Charles Marshall began the annual whitewashing of the tower in August 1900. Perched in a boatswain's chair suspended by ropes from the top of the lighthouse, Keeper Marshall was working at a height of forty-five feet when he discovered that the control rope for lowering or raising the chair was beyond his reach. Realizing the seriousness of his predicament, Marshall vigorously waved at passing fisherman, but they just returned his greeting and continued on. Sunburned and nearly delirious, Marshall lashed himself to the chair as the day drew to a close. A passing tug noticed the light was out and stopped to investigate. Keeper Marshall was lowered to the ground and taken to a doctor in Mackinaw City, but the effects of the ordeal remained with him the rest of his life. George Leggatt, an assistant at Old Mackinac Point Lighthouse, was sent to be the new head keeper at St. Helena Island, and Keeper Marshall was given Leggatt's former position, which required less responsibility.

Charles Marshall served as an assistant to his brother George at Old Mackinac Point until 1902, when his health deteriorated to the point that he had to be hospitalized at the Northern Michigan Asylum in Traverse City.

An account on the Mackinac State Historic Parks' website (MackinacParks.org) also noted: "In early April, according to George Marshall's official station logbook, Charles was 'adjudged insane and taken away to Traverse City,' where he was confined in the state mental hospital for the rest of his life. When Charles' wife, Rose, died in 1907, their children, Chester, Ethel and Nora, came to live at Old Mackinac Point with their uncle George and his wife Maggie, as well as their aunt Sara [*sic*] and her husband, assistant keeper William Barnum."

Official records note that Charles's last day of service was May 31, 1902, when he "resigned" from duty.

In the 1910 census of the Northern Michigan Asylum, Charles is listed as an "inmate," but by 1920, patients—at least in his ward—were considered "boarders." After twenty-four years of confinement within the massive Traverse City State Hospital complex, Charles died at the age of sixty-eight on August 12, 1926, of skin cancer (1920, 48) and tuberculosis of the respiratory system (1920, 31), according to his death certificate and the "International List of Causes of Death, Revision 3" list of 1920. He was buried at the Lakeview Cemetery in Mackinaw City, along with his brother William A. and sister, Mary, as well as several other members of the Marshall family.

Two of Charles and Rose's daughters died in childhood, including Olive (details about her death are unknown, although she was listed with the

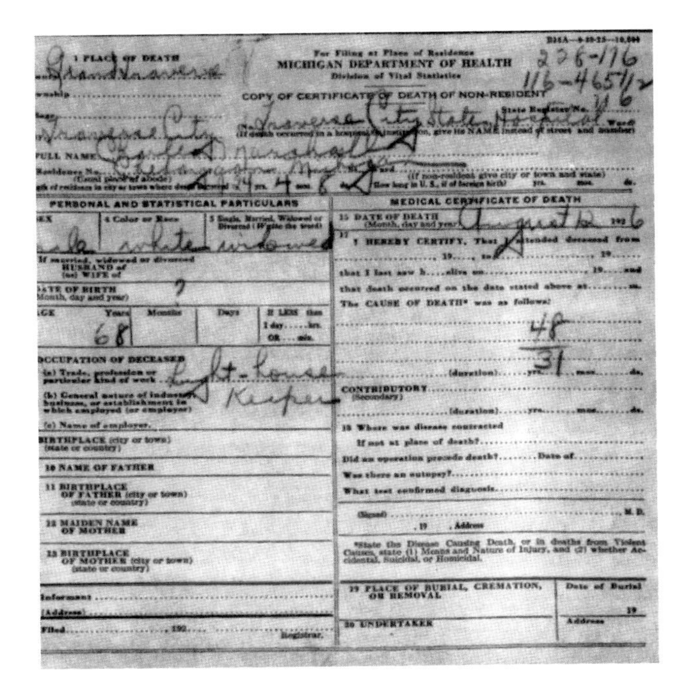

1 PLACE OF DEATH

Grand Traverse

For Filing at Place of Residence
MICHIGAN DEPARTMENT OF HEALTH
Division of Vital Statistics

226-116
116-4651/2

COPY OF CERTIFICATE OF DEATH OF NON-RESIDENT

Township

State Registered No. 46

Traverse City

No. Traverse City State Hospital Ward
(If death occurred in a hospital or institution, give its NAME instead of street and number)

FULL NAME Charles Marshall

Residence No. Cheboygan, Mich.
(Usual place of abode) (If non-resident give city or town and state)

Length of residence in city or town where death occurred 24 yrs. 4 mos. 6 ds. How long in U.S., if of foreign birth? yrs. mos. ds.

PERSONAL AND STATISTICAL PARTICULARS

Sex male | 4 Color or Race white | 5 Single, Married, Widowed or Divorced (Write the word) widowed

If married, widowed or divorced HUSBAND of (or) WIFE of

Date of Birth (Month, day and year) ?

Age Years 68 | Months | Days | If LESS than 1 day ... hrs. OR ... min.

Occupation of Deceased
(a) Trade, profession or particular kind of work Light-house Keeper
(b) General nature of industry, business, or establishment in which employed (or employer)
(c) Name of employer.

Birthplace (city or town) (state or country)

10 NAME OF FATHER

11 BIRTHPLACE OF FATHER (city or town) (state or country)

12 MAIDEN NAME OF MOTHER

13 BIRTHPLACE OF MOTHER (city or town) (state or country)

Informant

(Address)

Filed ... 192... Registrar.

MEDICAL CERTIFICATE OF DEATH

15 DATE OF DEATH (Month, day and year) August 12 1926

17 I HEREBY CERTIFY, That I attended deceased from ... 19..., to ... 19...

that I last saw h... alive on ... 19... and

that death occurred on the date stated above at ... m.

The CAUSE OF DEATH* was as follows:

48

31

(duration) ... yrs. ... mos. ... ds.

CONTRIBUTORY (Secondary)

(duration) ... yrs. ... mos. ... ds.

18 Where was disease contracted

If not at place of death?

Did an operation precede death? ... Date of.

Was there an autopsy?

What test confirmed diagnosis.

(Signed) ... M.D.

, 19 , Address

*State the Disease Causing Death, or in deaths from Violent Causes, state (1) Means and Nature of Injury, and (2) whether Accidental, Suicidal, or Homicidal.

19 PLACE OF BURIAL, CREMATION, OR REMOVAL | Date of Burial ... 19

20 UNDERTAKER | Address

Charles Marshall served as a lighthouse keeper in the Straits of Mackinac until he suffered a tragic accident that left him institutionalized at the Northern Michigan Asylum in Traverse City, where he ultimately died. *Courtesy of the State of Michigan.*

family on St. Helena Island in the 1900 census) and Jessie, who passed away on June 15, 1902, at the age of nine and was buried at the Saint Andrew Cemetery in Saginaw, Michigan. It is believed that Rose had family or friends in the "thumb" area of Michigan, given that it was not only where Jessie was buried but also where Chester was born. Nothing could be found on how Rose died or where she was buried.

As previously stated, Ethel, Nora and Chester were adopted by their aunts and uncles, but there was no mention of where fourteen-year-old Hazel ended up in 1907, after her mother's death. She later married John A. Howard from the Grand Rapids, Michigan area and lived until the age of ninety-four (passing away on May 2, 1992). Ethel married Elmer R. Robinson and remained in the Mackinaw area until her death at the age of eighty-four on December 3, 1978. Nora married Archie St. Germain but passed away at the age of thirty-nine on March 16, 1939.

Chester married Mary Ellen (Beneteaux) on October 17, 1930, in Mackinaw City, and they had two daughters. Like the Marshall men before him, Chester became a Great Lakes lighthouse keeper. His first appointment was as second assistant at the Beaver Head Island Lighthouse from 1935 to 1937. From there, he transferred to Wisconsin's Manitowoc North Breakwater, starting as a second assistant and being promoted in 1942 to first assistant. In 1963, he landed the title of principal keeper until his retirement in 1966, after more than thirty years of service.

Just two years after hanging up his hat, Chester's wife of thirty-eight years passed away. He, however, lived until a week past his seventy-sixth birthday, passing away on February 25, 1976. Both were buried in the Evergreen Cemetery in Manitowoc.

The restoration of the St. Helena Lighthouse is one of the greatest accomplishments of the Great Lakes Lighthouse Keepers Association (GLLKA) based in Mackinaw City. After the station was automated in the early 1920s and subsequently abandoned, the lighthouse fell into a severe state of disrepair at the hands of the four seasons in the Straits and, later, vandals (both humans and critters). In the early 1980s, GLLKA rallied its volunteers to raise awareness, money and hammers to restore the once-neglected light into a shining beacon. It is now open occasionally for public tours and has an active volunteer keeper program.

Access to St. Helena Island is offered during the summer out of Mackinaw City aboard the *Ugly Anne* through a partnership with GLLKA. The forty-minute boat ride travels through the Straits and under the Mackinac Bridge to the island. As the boat can only get so close to the shore (even in times of high-water levels), visitors are loaded into a small inflatable dingy to get to the island. There, volunteers are ready to greet guests at the dock, serve a picnic lunch and offer tours of the lighthouse, keeper's dwelling and boathouse. There are also walking trails around the island, but they are often saturated with water, and stepping off the paths is discouraged due to a high concentration of poison ivy.

5
POVERTY ISLAND LIGHTHOUSE

DELTA COUNTY, MICHIGAN

From its conception, Poverty Island and its now-abandoned lighthouse have been swathed in mystery, tragedy, death and legendary tales of kings, lost treasure and one of the Great Lakes' most infamous historic sailing vessels. It is ironic that in the 1870s—in a premonition of what was to come—the island and subsequent light would bear the name "Poverty," given their current state of neglect.

The two-hundred-acre island is located nearly six miles south of the Garden Peninsula in northern Lake Michigan at the mouth of the hazardous passage into Green Bay (the body of water, not the city), surrounded by Summer Island, Little Summer Island, Gravelly Island, Gull Island, Little Gull Island and St. Martin Island—the southernmost island in Michigan—all of which are contained within the Delta County footprint.

As early as the 1670s, this route was traversed by French explorers who were looking to make their mark in the fur trade industry. The most notable vessel to travel this route was *Le Griffon*, the first full-sized European sailing ship on the upper Great Lakes, commissioned and commanded by none other than René-Robert Cavelier, Sieur de La Salle. On the return trip of its maiden voyage, this forty-five-ton barque, adorned with a distinguishable carved griffon on the bow stem, disappeared with its entire crew of six and its cargo, including furs and seven cannons (at least two of which were said to be made of brass).

A number of stories about what happened on that fateful September day have been told over the years, including tales of storms that capsized the

One of the most notable vessels on the Great Lakes was *Le Griffon*, the first full-sized European sailing ship on the upper Great Lakes, commissioned and commanded by none other than René-Robert Cavelier, Sieur de La Salle. *From Google Images.*

boat, the vessel running aground on a shallow shoal, an ambush by local Natives and an inside job at the hands of the crew. Now, more than 340 years later, the real answer will likely never be uncovered; the exact location of this missing ship remains laden with speculation for both armchair and academic historians.

The coveted wreck of *Le Griffon* isn't the only sunken treasure believed to be in the waters around Poverty Island. Tales of four or five (or more) "chests full of gold" coins, bars and bullion valued at over $400 million located near the coastline or just offshore in the waters of Lake Michigan have been circulating for decades.

Some say that James Strang, the self-proclaimed Mormon king of Beaver Island (fifty-seven miles to the northeast), had pillaged the loot from his followers during his six-year reign from July 8, 1850, until his assassination on July 9, 1856. Had he tried to hide his horde, or was it stolen from him?

Why would he (or they) choose an island so far away when there are several closer to the Beaver Island Archipelago to stash the cache?

Another theory about the gold dates back to the Civil War, which ravaged the country from April 12, 1861, to April 19, 1865. A 2019 article in the *Green Bay Press-Gazette* recounts the story:

"According to the legend, Napoléon Bonaparte [Napoléon III, also known as Louis-Napoléon Bonaparte or Charles Louis-Napoléon Bonaparte (April 20, 1808–January 9, 1873), the first President of the French Republic and the only emperor of the Second French Empire] was desperate to assist the South during the Civil War. The production of cotton made the Confederacy's success of prime importance to the French leader. The story says several chests of gold, ironically also worth an approximate $400 million, were brought over land through Canada and loaded onto a schooner in Lake Michigan [where it was rumored to be further transported down the Mississippi River to Confederate leaders]. During its voyage, the ship was discovered and chased. The crew members chained the chests together and threw them overboard rather than risk the chance of being caught."

In March 2021, Brent Swancer posted an article under the headline "The Mysterious Lost Treasure of Poverty Island" on the website MysteriousUniverse.org. It provides more details of the rumored story.

"By some accounts, the ship was discovered by Union forces and sunk near Poverty Island, while others say it was dashed upon the rocks while attempting to make a misguided night run, and yet another version says they were attacked by French pirates. Whatever the case may be, the gold either went down with the ship or was hidden on the island in order to be collected later or even thrown overboard to keep it from being captured. At any rate, it was lost. In most versions of the tale, the chests, usually said to be five of them, were chained together, making it likely that if one is to find one, they will find all of them."

If the war chests were being sent from France, why wouldn't shipments be delivered to southern ports in states like North or South Carolina instead of taking the arduous trek through British-controlled eastern Canada, along the St. Lawrence Seaway, through the Great Lakes to the 336-mile-long Illinois Waterway and ultimately to the Mississippi? Why risk traveling through Union territory? In hindsight, if this story is fact versus fiction, clearly the chosen route was the wrong way to go. And given the secrecy of the mission at the time, there was no record or "news accounts" of any ships wrecking near Poverty Island in the 1860s.

It was during the Civil War that the region around northern Lake Michigan (also called "Grand Lac," "Lac des Illinois" and "Michi Gami") began to change dramatically, as mining industries took shape and communities were subsequently developed along the coastline.

Escanaba, the county seat of Delta County, was the name of a nineteenth-century Ojibwe village along the shores of Little Bay de Noc. Eli P. Royce founded a European-American port town of the same name here in 1863. A year later, a seventy-five-mile-long railroad line connecting Escanaba to Negaunee was completed to accommodate the growing iron ore industry. Trains could then transport their harvests south, to Lake Michigan, where they were loaded onto steamers headed toward Chicago, Detroit and points beyond. Those commercial vessels were welcomed into the harbor by the Sand Point Lighthouse, which had been put into service in 1868 (more information in chapter 6).

But getting into or out of port, through the island-riddled route toward Green Bay, remained a challenge and called for the construction of a lighthouse at the entrance of the dangerous passage. The October 17, 1867 issue of the *Buffalo Commercial* out of Buffalo, New York, reported, "By direction of the Light-house Board of the Treasury Department, the commissioner of the General Land Office has ordered the reservation for light-house purposes of Poverty Island, in Lake Michigan, embracing fractional sections 8 and 9, township 36, north of range 19 west, in the Marquette Land District."

A petition was subsequently filed, although it was an uphill battle getting the project to fruition. According to the 1867 "Report of the Secretary of Treasury" from Washington, D.C. (234): "The already large and rapidly increasing commerce to and from the northern end of Green Bay and lower lake ports now takes in daylight the northern passage from Lake Michigan into Green Bay, because of its being much shorter and more direct. To enable vessels to use the same passage in the night, a light-house on Poverty Island is necessary, and an estimate of the cost of building one is herewith submitted. The necessary reservation of the island for light-house purposes has been made."

The formal application was filed again in 1869, and by 1870, a dollar figure of $18,000 was added to the still-pending request. It wasn't until 1873, six years after the first submission, that the project was approved. The "Report of the Light-House Board (1870–1874)" noted (664) that finally "all the requisite preliminaries have been completed, and the erection of a light-house at this point, under the act of March 3, 1873, will be commenced before the close of this season."

In late August, the long and dreadful history of the Poverty Island Light Station officially began. Yet, just two months later, the construction of the tower and connecting keeper's dwelling was halted due to a late season fire, as reported in the "Report of the Light-House Board" (657–76):

"The construction of this light-house began August 28, 1873. The work was closed by a fire which commenced in the sleeping shanties while the men were at work, October 25, and which destroyed the temporary shelter and some material. Work with a small party was recommenced May 13 and was brought to a condition to permit of occupancy and the exhibition of a temporary light by the 14th of July, 1874, and then stopped for want of funds. The present condition of the station is as follows: The tower walls are up 31 feet from water table and covered. All steps and landings up with the walls, the plastering inside partly done. The dwelling is complete and painted and a wooden lantern erected on the roof for a temporary light, the lens for which will soon be set up. The completion of this light will cost about $3,000, for which an appropriation is asked."

The temporary light was perched on top of the keeper's house and was illuminated on September 1, 1874, as the final installment for additional funding wasn't approved until March 3, 1875. Later that spring, work on the tower resumed, and the permanent light—a fourth-order Fresnel lens—was eventually exhibited on August 10, 1875, according to the "Annual Report of the Secretary of the Treasury."

The light station included a conical brick tower with a decagonal cast-iron lantern room on top measuring seventy-feet tall connected to the one-and-a-half-story brick keeper's dwelling, all painted white. The design replicated that of the St. Helena Island Lighthouse (1873) in northern Lake Michigan and both the Sturgeon Point Lighthouse (1870) and Tawas Point Lighthouse (1876) on Lake Huron. (For more on St. Helena Island Lighthouse, see chapter 4.)

George Larson was named the first keeper of the Poverty Island light, starting his twenty-three-year career that also included Bailey's Harbor Rear Range, Racine Harbor and Little Fort/Waukegan Lights, all on Lake Michigan. He served in the head position at Poverty Island until 1882, drawing a salary of $600 a year. The station also employed both first and second assistant keepers, and during its nearly one hundred years of service, more than thirty men served there. During times when the keepers' wives and children were also on site, the island remained a busy yet remote locale.

The "gales of November" (and December) stirred up trouble for this new lighthouse in those early years under Larson's watch.

The construction of the Poverty Island Lighthouse began on August 28, 1873, but it faced several setbacks, including a fire and lack of funding, before it was put into operation. *Courtesy of Kraig Anderson and LighthouseFriends.com.*

The schooner *Dick Somers* met its end on Poverty Island in November 1877 and was a total loss according to Captain N.P. Hines. Three years later, in December 1880, the schooner *George H. Warmington* was said to have dragged its anchor from under the lee of Poverty Island when it became stranded on the reef between Big and Little Summer Islands (in 1878, this ship was also hung up on the Starve Island Reef in Lake Erie, near South Bass Island).

On November 24, 1881, a well-noted accident between two vessels from the New England Transportation Company led to the sinking of the propeller steam barge *Lake Erie* after it was struck by the *Northern Queen* during an early morning snowstorm. Hauling corn and sundries, the ships were traveling in tandem from Chicago to Collingwood in Ontario, Canada, as it was thought this would be safer than making the late-season trip alone. Sporting a large hole in its starboard side, the *Lake Erie* sank within one hundred minutes of the collision. Its crew boarded the *Northern Queen* to go to Manistique, about fifty miles to the northeast in Michigan's Upper Peninsula. Sadly, one deckhand named William Forbes, who had been scalded by steam when a pipe burst in the engine room on impact,

James M. McCormick was promoted and transferred to the Poverty Island Lighthouse in 1911 as head keeper. *Courtesy of Kraig Anderson and LighthouseFriends.com.*

died of his injuries. He was the only casualty out of a combined crew of nearly thirty men.

The *Northern Queen* fared better in the accident, but its fate was also doomed. The following morning, while trying to enter Manistique Harbor during yet another snow squall, the boat ran aground, going into the piers. It immediately began to fill with water and soon fell to pieces. Thankfully, the entire crew was able to vacate the sinking ship, escaping with nothing but the clothes on their backs.

The New England Transportation Company felt the full brunt of Lake Michigan's wrath that season, as it also lost the steamer *Columbia* and seventeen people on September 10, 1881, off the coast of Frankfort, Michigan.

Several upgrades were made to this island station over the course of its first dozen years, including the 1883 erection of a retaining wall around the foundation to support the tower cracked by the settling of the ground. "The boilers and machinery for a steam fog whistle to be established are under contract and will be established before the close of the navigation," said the 1885 report. Later, the 1895 report noted "a circular iron oil house was erected in September 1894. A boat landing was built in the shape of an L, so as to form a harbor for the keeper's boat. Additional crib was built to form a breakwater to the new landing."

In 1911, James M. McCormick was promoted and transferred from the Beaver Head Island Lighthouse (where he had served as second assistant keeper since 1904) to Poverty Island as principal keeper, effective September 15. His salary was a mere $624 annually, not much to support his pregnant wife, Mary Elizabeth (Wachter), and their growing family.

By the time they made their way to Poverty Island, the McCormicks had five children (two, William and Joseph, died as infants in 1901 and 1905, respectively). Three months (and two days) after her husband took over the helm of this light, Mary gave birth to Donald John, and in 1914, she gave birth to David Douglas "Doug," who would go on to serve in the coast guard in the Great Lakes region, at one time responsible for eighteen light stations on Lake Michigan in Michigan and Wisconsin. Five other children would follow, as Mary gave birth to twelve children between 1901 and 1923.

Less than a year into his service, McCormick narrowly escaped with his life after a freak accident aboard his lighthouse keeper's boat, as reported in the July 6, 1912 issue of the *Escanaba Morning Press*:

> *Jumping from his gasoline launch to escape the flames that were rapidly burning it to the water's edge, George* [incorrectly identifying James] *McCormick, the keeper of the lighthouse at Poverty Island, came very near to losing his life Wednesday afternoon.*
>
> *He had been to this city to do some shopping and was returning in the launch when in some unaccountable manner it got on fire.*
>
> *McCormick worked as long as he could to try and gain control of the flames and then finding that they were gaining headway rapidly, and that the tiny craft was doomed, he seized a life preserver and jumped over the side of the boat into the water.*
>
> *After drifting about for a considerable length of time he was picked up by a passing steamer and taken to his home on Poverty Island. The gasoline launch burned to the water's edge and then sank.*
>
> *The direct cause of the fire may never be known, but it is thought that there must have been a leak in the gasoline pipe and the escaping vapor was ignited by a spark from the engine, which might have been caused by a short circuit in the wiring.*

McCormick later transferred to the South Fox Island Lighthouse in 1915, serving there until 1923. At that time, he made his way to Grand Traverse Lighthouse near Cathead Bay in Northport, at the tip of Michigan's Leelanau Peninsula. He retired from the service in 1938 and passed away on December 21, 1952, at the age of seventy-nine. Mary lived until May 15, 1959. The two were buried at the Mount Carmel Cemetery in Manistee, Michigan.

The next keeper who was brought in to manage the Poverty Island Lighthouse was Niels (also spelled Nels) Peter Jensen (also spelled Jaensen). He was often referred to as N.P. Jensen and was born in Denmark in 1861. He began his keeper career in 1904 as a second assistant at the St. Joseph North Pierhead Light in southern Lake Michigan. He then spent ten years in assistant roles at the St. Martin Island Lighthouse (1905–15). Joining him at Poverty Island was his wife, Julia Ann Elizabeth (Wachter), the oldest sister of James McCormick's wife, Mary Elizabeth, and several of their nine children (born between 1895 and 1913).

One of Jensen's assistants was William H. Lee, who served a brief one-year stint of his five-year career at this island lighthouse. Born in Vermont in

1866, "Billy" Lee lived in Door County, Wisconsin (Washington Island), with his second wife, Lillie Esther Pearl (Ellis), and their children, four of whom were from his first marriage to Nikoline (Olson) and two of whom were Lillie's. Hired as an assistant keeper in the spring of 1923, Lee spent his time between the island and the mainland. That summer, he made a cheerful trip to pick up his wife and children for an extended stay at the lighthouse. A *Door County News* article, published on June 28, 1923, gave specific details about the hours leading up to Lee's heartbreaking death:

> *Death stalked in the wake of the happy union of William Lee and his family on Thursday and parted them a few hours after the joyous greeting.*
>
> *Mr. Lee is the assistant light keeper on Poverty Island, located about twenty miles north of here, and his heart was light and happy at the knowledge that he was to meet his wife here and take her to the lonesome island for a couple of months visit during the summer months, after a separation since he entered on his duties early in the spring.*
>
> *When Mrs. Lee and her two children arrived at the Washington Harbor dock shortly before noon on Thursday she was greeted by her husband, who had come from the light station in a motorboat to meet her. He seemed to be in excellent health and was radiant with happiness to meet his family and the anticipation of their company for the summer on that out-of-the-way and lonely place, which is inhabited by the lightkeepers only.*
>
> *Three hours after leaving Washington Harbor they arrived at their destination and with the assistance of Mr. Johnson, the second assistant lightkeeper, busied themselves in carrying the trunks and luggage of Mrs. Lee from the boat to the lighthouse. It being a very hot day, Mr. Lee told his wife that he felt a trifle ill and would go into the bathroom for a few minutes.*
>
> *After waiting for a reasonable length of time they called to him and receiving no answer to the calls, Mr. Johnson got a ladder and looked thru* [sic] *the window from the outside and was horrified to see Mr. Lee lying on the floor. The door was forced open and they discovered that he was dead, death having been apparently instantaneous.*

Another article that day in the *Green Bay Press-Gazette* shared more about the hours and days after Lee's death, as keeper Jensen instructed his other assistant, Benjamin Johnson, to take Lee's body to nearby Washington Island for burial.

"Johnson was a stranger about the waters adjacent to the island, and a heavy fog that increased in thickness with his departure made his trip a

MARGIN RESERVED FOR BINDING

WRITE PLAINLY, WITH UNFADING INK—THIS IS A PERMANENT RECORD.

MICHIGAN DEPARTMENT OF HEALTH
Division of Vital Statistics
CERTIFICATE OF DEATH

21 303

1 PLACE OF DEATH
County Delta, Mich.
Township Fairbanks
Village Poverty Isle
City
Registered No. 3

2 FULL NAME William H. Lee
a) Residence No. 526 N. Court

PERSONAL AND STATISTICAL PARTICULARS
3 SEX Male
4 Color or Race White
5 Single, Married, Widowed or Divorced Married
6 DATE OF BIRTH June 28th 1866
7 AGE 56 Years 11 Months 23 Days
8 OCCUPATION OF DECEASED Assistant Light House Keeper
(c) Name of employer U. S. Government
9 BIRTHPLACE State of Vermont
10 NAME OF FATHER
11 BIRTHPLACE OF FATHER
12 MAIDEN NAME OF MOTHER
13 BIRTHPLACE OF MOTHER
14 Informant Mrs. Wm H. Lee
(Address) Sturgeon Bay, Wis.
15 Filed July 23 1923 Emma Foll... Registrar

MEDICAL CERTIFICATE OF DEATH
16 DATE OF DEATH June 21 1923
17 I HEREBY CERTIFY, That I attended deceased from
The CAUSE OF DEATH was as follows:
acute dilatation of heart
(Signed) D. ... Barclay
Escanaba
19 PLACE OF BURIAL, CREMATION, OR REMOVAL Washington Isle, Wis.
Date of Burial 6/23/1923
20 UNDERTAKER

William Lee was an assistant keeper at the Poverty Island Lighthouse when he died suddenly in the summer of 1923. *Courtesy of the State of Michigan.*

perilous one. After running a sufficient length of time to reach his destination, Mr. Johnson was alarmed evidently having taken the wrong course. The boat continued on its way with its dead passenger until it grounded. The trip being made in the dead of night, the boatman did not know where he struck. With dawn the fog lifted he found that he was many miles off his course, grounded on Fisherman's Shoals.

"With some difficulty he freed the boat and reached Washington Harbor. Leaving the body of his mate with friends, he returned to Poverty Island to get the distracted widow and children, and bring them back for the funeral. In the meanwhile, Captain Jepsen [*sic*] received relief from narby [*sic*] St. Martin's Island.

"Funeral services were conducted Saturday at Washington Island by Rev. John Malloch of the Bethel church.

"William Lee was 57 years old and hda [*sic*] been a resident of Door County for 30 years. He had been in the government lighthouse service since 1918, previously being stationed at Twin River Point [Rawley Point, 1918–19] and Pilot Island [1919–22]. He was transferred to Poverty Island this spring.

"He is survived by his widow, three daughters and a son by his first marriage, and two stepchildren."

The run of bad luck for keepers at Poverty Island was not over, although four years would pass before the next incident of note. At the end of the 1927 season, keepers Jensen, Johnson and Jessen were preparing to vacate the island to spend the winter on Washington Island with their respective families, but Mother Nature had a different idea, as reported in the December 14, 1927 issue of the *Green Bay Press-Gazette*:

"Three men who were marooned in the Poverty Island Lighthouse by last week's storms were here today, saved by the fishing boat Silver Spray, Fairport, Mich. They are Keeper N.P. Jensen and Ben Johnson, Marinette and Abe Jessen, Washington Island.

"Their plans to leave the lighthouse Dec. 7 were blocked by the storm. Uable [*sic*] to reach the mainland in their small boat, they existed on half rations until only a box of crackers and three tame rabbits were left.

"Telephone communication failed them, but by use of the foghorn, they attracted the Silver Spray, which cut through three miles of ice to reach their island."

Jensen and Jessen would face another mishap on October 23, 1936, while on nearby Washington Island—one that would leave one of the men dead. The *Door County Advocate*, on October 30 that year, noted that the situation involving the keepers was one of two fatal island traffic accidents within a forty-eight-hour period.

"The first death was that of Nels Peter Jensen, 64, keeper of the Poverty Island lighthouse, who was struck by a car driven by Arnie Richter while walking with Abe Jessen to the annual school board convention at Nelson's Hall [a legendary establishment opened by Tom Nelson in 1899, which survived Prohibition by serving medicinal 90-proof Angostura bitters, which is still served today].

"After learning the facts regarding the Jensen death, Coroner [Calmer] Nelson decided that no inquest was necessary. Mr. Jensen, it was said, was the victim of confusion in trying to get out of the road. According to reports, he started across the highway when he saw the car coming and then turned back into the path of the machine. Mr. Richter was freed of all blame in connection with the accident. The body was prepared for burial by the Casperson Funeral Home of Sister Bay, and on Sunday, it was taken to the home of a daughter, Bertha, at Fayette, Mich., by the Plum Island coast guards [*sic*]. Services were held there Monday. The family home is at Marinette but Mrs. Jensen was living with her husband on the island for the season."

Jensen was buried in the Hinks Cemetery in Fayette (Delta County), along with his wife, Julia, who passed away on June 19, 1942.

Following Jensen's death, Benjamin Johnson moved up to the principal keeper position. He had originally arrived on Poverty Island in 1921 and worked his way up the ranks, serving until 1943. Only a handful of other men worked at this post in its final years.

The coast guard removed the Fresnel lens in 1950 and replaced it with a modern tower. By 1957, the station was fully automated, and its keeper service was discontinued. Left abandoned, the dwelling, outbuildings and tower were subjected to the damaging effects of the seasons, and ultimately, vandals contributed to its ruin.

The light was converted to solar power atop a skeletal steel tower near the middle of the island in 1976. The cast-iron lantern room was removed shortly thereafter, and it was stored on the island until it was donated to the Delta County Historical Society in Escanaba for the restoration of the Sand Point Lighthouse (see more in chapter 6). Brush overgrowth forced the solar-powered light to be moved once again, back to the top of the brick tower (sans lantern room), where it stayed perched for another ten years or so before it was permanently extinguished in 1995.

Interest in Poverty Island and its treasured history has remained a constant over the past century. A 2019 *Green Bay Press-Gazette* article went on to mention an incident that occurred in the early 1920s, when an unnamed freighter ran aground and the tugboats that were sent to drag it off the rocks inadvertently snagged some wooden boxes chained together with its anchors. "However, as the wooden boxes were brought to the surface, the chests broke free and returned to the watery depths."

A few years later, a young Carl Jessen, the son of one-time assistant keeper Abraham Jessen, reportedly observed men on a salvage boat offshore searching for something. Having heard of the lost treasure chests, Carl suspected that's exactly what the men were trying to find. "Suddenly, a storm descended on them, almost as if to deny them the treasure. In the storm, the salvage boat was lost." That salvage boat was later determined to be the *Captain Lawrence*, which became stranded on September 19,

1933, and fell beneath the shallow waters to rest about fifty feet below the lake's surface.

Steven Libert, a self-proclaimed treasure hunter, began diving in the area around Poverty Island in the early 1980s, searching for answers. He reportedly found two items (an anchor and a propeller blade) that he believed belonged to the *Captain Lawrence*. Libert is one of a handful of noted historians on the quest to solve the mystery of this Civil War gold—not to be confused with the History Channel show *The Curse of Civil War Gold*, which aired two seasons (2018–19) and was centered around Frankfort, Michigan.

The story of the sunken treasure near Poverty Island reached a broader audience when the television show *Unsolved Mysteries* arrived in the area in 1994. It followed the lead of Richard Bennett, a professional diver and author of "The Poverty Island Sunken Treasure Brief," who has reportedly spent forty-five years and over $100,000 on his personal quest to uncover the treasure. Even that show left without uncovering anything new.

Theories surrounding *Le Griffon* have also resurfaced in recent years. In the summer of 2013, U.S. and French archaeologists began a joint operation to examine an underwater artifact that was found near Poverty Island to determine its possible connection to the lost 1670s vessel, but nothing of significance has been reported since that initial investigation began (as of the fall of 2021).

The Poverty Island Lighthouse is one of about ten Great Lakes lights on the "Doomsday List of Endangered Lighthouses" compiled by *Lighthouse Digest*. *Courtesy of Mike and Carol McKinney.*

Over time, the Poverty Island Lighthouse continued to deteriorate, falling into a state of disrepair. *Lighthouse Digest* even added it to its "Doomsday List of Endangered Lighthouses" in 2011. The list draws attention to lights that are in such a state of deterioration that they're in danger of being lost forever if efforts aren't made to preserve them. Currently, about forty lights are on the list, ten in the Great Lakes region.

"The scene that presents itself today at the old light station is one of the most pitiful on the Great Lakes," said author Wayne S. Sapulski in an article he wrote for the spring 2011 issue of the *Beacon*, a publication of the Great Lakes Lighthouse Keepers Association, based in Mackinaw City, Michigan.

"The rocky site is wildly overgrown. The decapitated lighthouse is in an advanced state of decay. Paint is peeling, bricks are spalling, and the interior is unsafe to enter. A quilt-work of rotting plywood patches placed by concerned individuals over the years covers some of the many holes in the roof that have allowed water seepage to compromise the structural integrity of the building. The assistant keeper's dwelling next door has already collapsed in on itself. The dock, boathouse and fog signal building are all gone. The only other structure remaining at the site, the cast-iron oil house, is severely corroded."

And that was before a devastating wildfire scorched the deserted island in 2016. A lightning strike on June 26 set the dry brush around the island ablaze, and area agencies banded together to help extinguish it, returning on occasion throughout the summer and fall to handle flare-ups.

On Monday, August 8, the island's Fire Incident Command Team noted that about 25 percent (or fifty acres) of the island had burned by that point. Jeremy Bennett, a U.S. Bureau of Indian Affairs firefighter, reported that a sprinkler system was set up to protect the lighthouse and crews were "strategically burning out debris in an area around it and other buildings in order to protect them from the wildfire."

According to a September 2016 statement from the Bureau of Indian Affairs (BIA): "A boat loaned from Apostle Islands National Lakeshore, a U.S. Forest Service helicopter and firefighters from the BIA, Fish and Wildlife Service and Forest Service are assisting in the management efforts. The fire is burning in peat and heavy-standing and blown-down timber, vegetation that will cause the fire to smolder until winter weather eventually puts the fire out. Until that time, firefighters are taking action to protect the lighthouse and surrounding buildings. Once structures are protected, firefighters will monitor the fire until winter finishes their job."

The fire was smoldering and kicking up well into the fall, with smoke visible in northwest Lower Michigan, the Upper Peninsula and even parts of Wisconsin.

In 2005, Poverty Island Light Station was listed in the National Register of Historic Places. The island itself is currently owned in its entirety by the U.S. Coast Guard, which is in the process of transferring the undeveloped portion of the island to the U.S. Fish and Wildlife Service. At that time, it will become a unit of the Green Bay National Wildlife Refuge (along with Pilot and Plum Islands northeast of Door County, Wisconsin). That process is expected to take about three years. The coast guard will retain ownership of the Poverty Island Lighthouse and Light Station grounds.

6

SAND POINT LIGHTHOUSE

ESCANABA, MICHIGAN

The Lake Michigan shoreline town of Escanaba holds a dark secret—an unsolved mystery, dating back to 1886, involving the death of one of Michigan's most notable female lighthouse keepers: Mary Terry.

Incorporated in 1862, Escanaba's early lumbering and fishing industries brought vessels into the area on a regular basis, thus warranting the need for a lighthouse within its first two years. Congress appropriated $5,000 for a beacon to be built at Escanaba's Sand Point, named for the location on which it stood, but issues in securing a clean title to the property from the original landowner delayed the project. An additional $9,000 was allocated in 1867 to finally construct the story-and-a-half brick building outfitted with a cast-iron lantern room and a fourth-order Fresnel lens operated with a fixed red signal.

According to TerryPepper.com, the fourth-order Fresnel lens was the most commonly used lens around the Great Lakes. With a focal plane of forty-four feet above the surrounding water and a range of up to fifteen nautical miles, these nearly twenty-nine-inch-tall crystal-like lenses weighed between 440 and 660 pounds, consuming about five and one-quarter ounces of oil (whale oil, lard or, later, kerosene) per hour to produce their prismed light.

Interestingly, the Sand Point Lighthouse was built 180 degrees off from the original plan; the forty-one-foot-tall tower sat closer to town on the west side of the building, instead of closer to Little Bay de Noc to the east. One can only wonder how far along in the process the contractors were when they realized the error and if anyone lost their job or was held responsible for the noteworthy mistake.

This pencil drawing is the only known image of John Terry, the first appointed keeper of the Sand Point Lighthouse in Escanaba. He died before he could take command of his post. *Courtesy of the Delta County Historical Society.*

With construction well under way, it was time to find a suitable keeper.

John Terry was born on August 6, 1818, on the eastern coast of Canada (some note St. Johns, which is the capital of Newfoundland and Labrador Provinces, and others note the neighboring province of New Brunswick). On February 21, 1845, Terry wed Mary L. Thurston, born in 1816 to Samuel and Elizabeth (Gifford) Thurston (sometimes published Thursdon) in Dartmouth, Massachusetts.

In June 1863, the Peninsula Division of the Chicago & North-Western Railway broke ground on the construction of the line between Escanaba and Negaunee. John was hired as a surveyor, and he and Mary, who had been married for just over twenty-four years with no children, moved to the Upper Peninsula. Years later, in the 1883 publication *History of the Upper Peninsula of Michigan*, it was noted that John "was in the employ of the Chicago & North-Western Railroad Company on the surveying and construction of the line and was one of the first men who did business on the dock; he was with the company for some years."

On November 4, 1867, a brief in the *Buffalo Commercial* out of New York read "The *Green Bay Advocate* says that Capt. John Terry, known to the bay and rivermen, has been appointed keeper of the new lighthouse at Escanaba. Work on the building is progressing rapidly, twenty-five to thirty men being employed on it. It is located on the extremity of Sand Point. The walls are of Escanaba brick, faced with those of Milwaukee manufacture."

Official keeper records cataloged by Phyllis L. Tag of the Great Lakes Research Project note that Captain Terry's official appointment took place on December 19, 1867, for the annual salary of $540. Given that it was wintertime, as would have been customary for that time of year, the light was left dormant and was illuminated for the first time the following spring. Yet John would never fire up that light, as he died on April 8, 1868 (at the age of forty-nine), of consumption (tuberculosis). He was buried at the Lakeview Cemetery on Third Avenue South in Escanaba.

The *Detroit Free Press* reported on May 1, 1868: "We were much pained to learn from a contemporary the death of our old shipmate and friend,

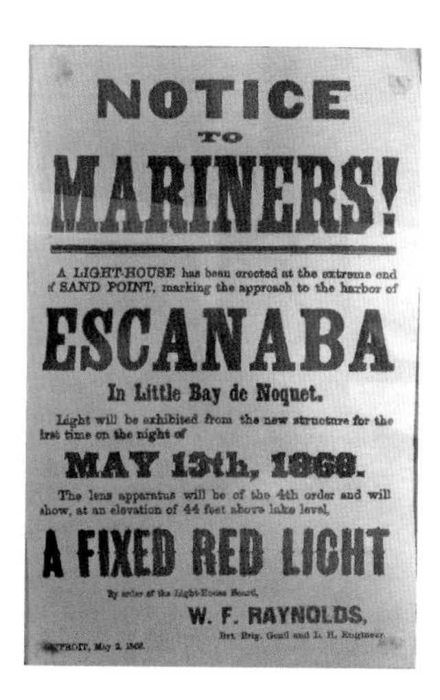

NOTICE
TO
MARINERS!
A LIGHT-HOUSE has been erected at the extreme end of SAND POINT, marking the approach to the harbor of
ESCANABA
In Little Bay de Noquet.
Light will be exhibited from the new structure for the first time on the night of
MAY 13th, 1868.
The lens apparatus will be of the 4th order and will show, at an elevation of 44 feet above lake level,
A FIXED RED LIGHT
W. F. RAYNOLDS,

The Sand Point Lighthouse in Escanaba was put into service on May 13, 1868. *Courtesy of the U.S. Lighthouse Society.*

Capt. John Terry, at Green Bay, where, for several years past, he had been plying his vocation in command of a steamer, though of late in charge of a lighthouse in that locality. Mr. Terry was true-hearted a sailor as ever paced the deck and for many years was connected with steamers plying between Buffalo and Green Bay and was long a resident of Buffalo."

At that point, John's widow, Mary, requested to serve in his stead. It is said there was strong opposition from Washington, D.C., where the U.S. Lighthouse Service was based. However, her application was so strongly endorsed that the inspectors finally agreed.

She followed in the footsteps of only a handful of women before her when she fulfilled the obligations as head keeper, with an official appointment on April 18. The light was officially put into service on May 13. Her salary was the same amount her husband would have been paid—$540 annually. As it turns out, it was pretty customary for female lighthouse keepers to be paid the same rate as their male counterparts, which is surprising given it was a government job in the nineteenth century.

Unlike other Great Lakes light keepers, Mary never enlisted the help of an assistant keeper. So, day in and day out, year after year, she diligently and faithfully took care of her beacon. It was a position she grew fond of, one that she became well-respected for and one that would pay her nearly $10,000 over her eighteen years of service. Mary invested some of that money into buying a handful of lots around Escanaba between 1883 and 1885; the rest of her funds were stashed away inside the lighthouse. It was a dream job that Mary would die for—literally. In the overnight hours of March 5, 1886, a fire broke out at Sand Point Lighthouse, consuming the entire structure and Mary herself. What really happened that night is a mystery that likely only she knows. The theories are plenty, including everything from a simple furnace fire to foul play. Some local legends tell a sinister story involving a break-in, murder and cover-up.

One account says that a robber kicked in the door to the lower-level storage room of the lighthouse to the right of the tower with thoughts of robbing the keeper, a widowed woman who was known to hoard her money within the confines of her home. An astute Mary awoke after hearing the clatter and made her way from her bedroom in the opposite corner on the upper floor to the basement, where she encountered the intruder. A struggle ensued, and Mary, unable to defend herself, was killed. The fire, it is said, was started to make her death look like an accident.

Several newspapers wrote about the accident, from California and Montana to Arkansas and Pennsylvania (more than fifty individual outlets based on a search through Newspapers.com). Locally, the front page of the *Iron Port*, a weekly Escanaba paper, was one of the first to cover the accident and published this report the day of Mary's death:

> *The lighthouse on Sand Point was destroyed by fire on the morning of Friday. Just the time when the fire was started, it was impossible to say, but when the alarm was given, at about one o'clock, the flames had entire possession of the building and had broken through the roof, and nothing could be done either to save it or its contents. It was known that the keeper Mrs. Mary L. Terry occupied the building, and, as she was not seen or heard from, it was at once apprehended that she perished in the house, and when the subsidence of the fire and the coming of daylight made an examination of the ruins possible, these fears were changed to certainties by the discovery of her remains therein. Mrs. Terry has had charge of the light nearly 18 years. She was a very methodical woman, very careful in the discharge of her duties and very particular in the care of the property under her charge, and it is difficult to believe that the fire was accidental. She was economical and, out of her salary, has saved enough to purchase some property in the city; was reputed a woman of means, to a certain extent, and it is easier to believe that the burning of the house and her death is the outcome of a scheme of robbery than to believe it an accident. Justice Glaser and a coroner's jury composed of P. Coffee, C.J. Provo, S.F. Edwards, Henry McFall, Chas. H. Scott and John Lawrence viewed the remains (mere fragments—a portion of the skull, a few bones and a small portion of the viscera), which were then placed in charge of D.A. Oliver and an adjournment taken to give time for the collection of evidence. The furnace by which the house was heated was in bad order, and it is not impossible that the fire originated there. Bordman Leighton, who was employed about the place, on Thursday, noticed that the wood near it was hot and called Mrs. Terry's attention to it, to which she replied that she expected to be burned out by it someday but added that she slept with one eye open. The remains were not found in the ruins of her bedroom, which*

was on the north side of the house, but in the southeast corner, evidence pretty conclusive that she did not perish in her bed, unwarned. Mrs. Terry was about 69 years of age.

That same day, the *Chicago Tribune* included a brief, which read "Destruction of the Escanaba Lighthouse—Its Female Keeper Perishes in the Flames": "The Escanaba Lighthouse burned about 1 o'clock this morning. The lightkeeper, Mrs. Mary L. Terry, perished in the building. The origin of the fire is unknown. It is believed to have caught from the furnace and to have been burning inside for some time before discovery and that Mrs. Terry suffocated before the flames broke through. Nothing remains but the brick walls and the light-tower, which is brick and iron. It is a noteworthy fact that Mrs. Terry exhibited the first light after the completion of the house on May 13, 1868, and has ever since held the position of keeper."

The *Nebraska State Journal* also published a short story under the headline "Burned in a Lighthouse": "The lighthouse on the Sand Point of Escanaba was destroyed by fire this morning. When the fire was discovered about one o'clock, nothing could be done to save the building or contents, as the flames were bursting from the roof windows and doors. Mrs. Mary G. Terry, lightkeeper, perished in the house. The fire is supposed to have caught from the furnace, as it was in bad order. Others advance robbery, as Mrs. Terry was a woman of means and lived alone. Only a small portion of the skull and a few bones were recovered. The lighthouse was completed in 1868, and Mrs. Terry has had charge ever since. She was 69 years of age."

The website LighthouseFriends.com offered another account from the Lighthouse Board of the situation: "The light-keeper was burned to death and the station damaged by a fire, which originated in the dwelling on the night of March 4, 1886. The woodwork and stone caps and sills of the buildings were destroyed, but the brickwork and metalwork of the dwelling and tower were left comparatively uninjured. The damage was repaired as soon as practicable, the work having been commenced on April 1 and finished on May 31. The light was shown on the opening of navigation. The actual cost of the repairs was $2,362.72.

"As part of a six-man jury appointed to investigate the cause of Mary Terry's death, a handyman named Bordman Leighton testified that he had done some work for the keeper the day before she died and had warned her about some firewood stored too near a furnace. Keeper Terry reportedly replied that she 'expected to be burned out by it someday,' but 'slept with one eye open' to improve her chances. An article in the local newspaper

On the night of March 6, 1886, the door to the lower level of the Sand Point Lighthouse, pictured here, was kicked in, and a subsequent fire contributed to the death of keeper Mary Terry. *Author's collection.*

described Mary as 'a very methodical woman, very careful in the discharge of her duties and very particular in the care of the property under her charge.' Some believe that there might have been foul play involved, as the dwelling's south door had its bolt shot forward as though the door had been forced, but Mary's modest fortune of $4,000 in gold coins was found in the lighthouse."

Whether the fire that took Mary's life and decimated the Sand Point Lighthouse was an accident or intentionally set, there were other factors at play that fateful night. Given that the blaze broke out in the first week of March, snow on the ground may have hampered men from accessing the light to douse the flames.

Escanaba didn't have weather observers in 1886, according to the National Oceanic and Atmospheric Administration, but reports from Marquette (sixty-six miles to the north) were archived. Although no snow accumulation totals are available, it appears Marquette received just over twenty-eight inches of snow in January and nearly ten inches of snow in February. Temperatures in the first week of March were relatively normal, with lows in the teens and highs around 30 degrees Fahrenheit. Locals, however, said there was enough snow on the ground to impact the volunteer, horse-drawn fire department from accessing the light.

According to *History of the Upper Peninsula in Delta County, Michigan*: "The first fire company was organized in 1867 by Master Mechanic Kilpatrick of the Chicago & North-Western Railway, who was elected foreman. It was furnished with buckets, a few hooks and was organized principally for the protection of the property of the Chicago & North-Western Railway Company. A short time after, the company purchased one of the old steamers of the Chicago Fire Department, which did service for a number of years."

It was in the spring of 1873 (about eighteen months after the "great fires" that devastated Chicago, as well as Peshtigo, Wisconsin, and Holland, Manistee and Port Huron, Michigan) when Escanaba established its first official fire department.

"Escanaba Fire Company No. 1 was organized on March 15, 1873, and, on the 22nd of March, adopted its rules and regulations. Steamer No. 1 arrived at Escanaba on May 31, 1873, and at a special meeting held at this date, twenty-five members volunteered their services as firemen, signing the constitution and by-laws previously framed, effecting a permanent organization of the company.…The steamer is a fourth-class engine of the Clapp & Jones manufacturer, having a power of throwing 300 gallons per minute.

The volunteer fire department in Escanaba, circa 1880. *Courtesy of the Delta County Historical Society.*

"It is furnished with three hose carts, carrying 1,700 feet of hose. Water is kept hot in a boiler by a Silsby heater, and although the facilities for hauling it to and from fires are not the best and quickest, yet when once in operation, it does good work and has saved much valuable property during its years of service in the village.

"The company has thirty-five members at this time and is exceedingly well-drilled for a volunteer company....The property of the company consists of an ordinary village truck, furnished with four Holloway chemical engines, two extension ladders, one forty-six feet long, the other thirty-six feet; one eighteen-foot ladder and two scaling ladders. The other implements comprise hooks, axes, crowbars and six fire buckets. The men are well-drilled and thoroughly understand their duties.

"The engine house is a large frame building, the ground floor being occupied for the repository of the steamer, hose carts and hook-and-ladder truck, while the second floor is furnished as a spacious hall, appropriately decorated for the various business meetings of the companies."

Yet despite all this equipment and a crew of able-bodied men, the Sand Point Lighthouse was a complete loss.

During its seventy-two-year history, just nine people served as lighthouse keepers at Sand Point. In 1939, when the light was decommissioned, the property was transferred to the U.S. Coast Guard (as were countless other sites around the Great Lakes during that era). During that transition, a crib light was built offshore to fulfill the navigational needs of mariners. That light remains active to this day.

Around that time, major structural changes were also made to the original lighthouse and its grounds—most notably the removal of the lens, spiral metal stairway and lantern room, as well as a reduction of the tower's height by ten feet. Poor Sand Point lost its lighthouse look. Additional modifications included raising the roof four feet to allow for the construction of three bedrooms and a bathroom on the second floor for the officer-in-charge of the aids to navigation team, who was to reside there with his family. Holes were cut into the walls to accommodate more windows and doors, and eventually, the beautiful brick exterior was covered in sheet insulation and aluminum siding.

In the mid-1980s, about one hundred years after the structure was rebuilt, Sand Point Lighthouse was about to undergo another major overhaul, this time to return it to its original stature. The Delta County Historical Society saved the building from possible leveling by the coast guard and began raising money and awareness for one of the area's oldest and most historic structures.

Thankfully, copies of the original 1867 plans were found, and the society went to work restoring, repairing and rebuilding Escanaba's beloved lighthouse. Two major architectural elements—a cast-iron lantern room unit and a fourth-order Fresnel lens—were obtained from the Poverty Island Lighthouse and Menominee Pier Light, respectively, to complete the project. The interior was then decorated to reflect the style at the turn of the nineteenth century, and after five years of sweat, laughter and tears, Sand Point Lighthouse opened to the public as a museum in 1990. Ownership of the light was eventually transferred to the society in 1998.

Given the rareness, fragility and value of Fresnel lenses, coupled with the fact that thousands of people climb the tower each year, the society commissioned Artworks Florida to build and install a replica lens in the tower in 2014. The original lens was then moved to the Delta County Historical Society Museum, next to the lighthouse, where it sits proudly on display.

Sand Point Lighthouse is open seasonally (Memorial Day weekend through Labor Day weekend) for tours, including the opportunity to climb to the top of the tower.

7
PILOT ISLAND LIGHTHOUSE

DOOR COUNTY, WISCONSIN

Isolation—both physical and emotional—possibly led to the 1880 self-inflicted death of a keeper at the Pilot Island Lighthouse, located northeast of Door County, Wisconsin.

The Lake Michigan waters around Door County are home to thirty-five islands, most of which are inaccessible. Among the more noted are Rock Island, Detroit Island, Pilot Island, Plum Island and Washington Island, which was once called *Wassekiganesco*, an Ojibwe name that translates to "his breast is shining" in reference to the reflection of the sun off the nearby limestone cliffs. With more than three hundred miles of rocky shoreline, the Door County Peninsula is also home to nearly a dozen lighthouses.

The first light at Ports des Morts (meaning "Death's Door" or "Door of the Dead"), which separates Door County along Green Bay in northeastern Wisconsin from Michigan's southwestern Upper Peninsula at the Garden Peninsula, was constructed on the southern end of Plum Island in 1848 for $3,500. It was short-lived, surviving just ten years before a new light was built two miles away on the equally remote Pilot Island. This location was surrounded by numerous shoals: "a naturally submerged ridge, bank or bar that consists of or is covered by sand or other unconsolidated material and rises from the bed of a body of water to near the surface," according to *Merriam-Webster*. Essentially, a "sandbar."

The United States Lighthouse Board, the second agency of the U.S. Federal Government's Department of Treasury, operated between 1851 and 1910. The earliest lighthouse keeper appointments came from the office

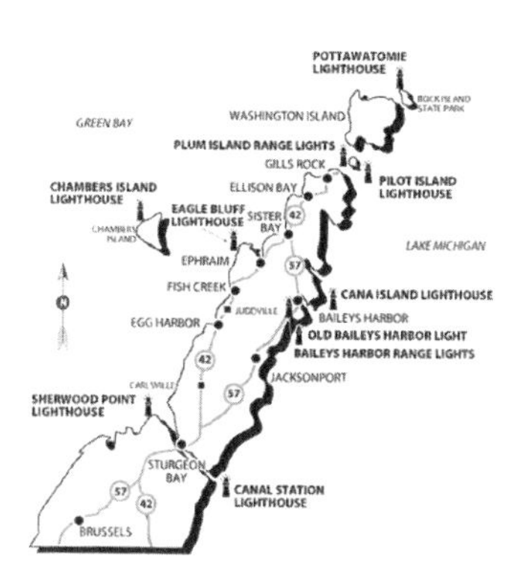

Door County is rich with Great Lakes shoreline, islands and historic lighthouses. *Courtesy of Destination Door County.*

of the president—from Washington to Jefferson—and eventually became a task of the secretary of the treasury. James Buchanan Jr., the fifteenth president of the United States, reserved the 3.7-acre Pilot Island for a new light, and the highest point, some eleven feet above the waters of Lake Michigan, was selected as the specific location for this 1858 beacon.

The two-story rectangular lighthouse on Pilot Island was constructed using a locally produced "Milwaukee brick," which was made from clay harvested from the Menominee River Valley. Regarded as more resilient than traditional red bricks, this yellow- or cream-colored clay's mixture was naturally high in magnesia and lime, giving it its unique color and durability according to Andrew Charles Stern, author of the 2015 thesis "Cream City: The Brick that Made Milwaukee Famous." In fact, by the time this light was constructed, Milwaukee was dubbed the "Cream City," based on its growing brick-production industry.

Dozens of men served at the Pilot Island Lighthouse over the years, with as many as three families living inside the large home at certain times. In 1876, Tobias Emanuel (referred to as Emanuel, Emmanuel or T.E.) Davidson and his wife, Christine Elizabeth (Markasun), moved into the light when he was named first assistant. He was soon promoted, earning a salary of $600 a year—his wife was his first assistant.

On October 1 of that year, John Marvin Boyce (also printed Baice, Baise, Bice, Boice and Boyse) was named second assistant keeper at a rate of $390 annually, replacing Byron Olson, who had resigned. Boyce was born in 1850 in Ontario, Canada, the second of three sons to John and Lucinda (Adams) Boyce. The first national census in 1851 featured some interesting notations regarding this family.

In Bayham, north of Lake Erie, there is a record of a twenty-eight-year-old farmer named John Baice living with his twenty-three-year-old wife, Lusindia (or Lucinda), and sons, William Amos (or Ames, also sometimes listed as Abraham), age three; and John, age one; as well as sixteen-year-old Loueza Adams (likely Lucinda's younger sister). That same year, a bit northeast, in Waterloo County, a twenty-three-year-old Lusindia Boyce and her two sons, William and John, ages three and one, respectively, are listed below other members of the Adams family (including a sixteen-year-old Loueza). There is no mention of a husband, and in fact, Lucinda is noted as a *spinster*—a term of the era referring to an older unmarried woman or a divorced younger woman.

However, two years later, in 1853, John and Lusindia welcomed their third son, Chauncey Abraham (also published Abidham or Obidham). Sadly, their family of five was broken up the following year, when their patriarch passed away. John was buried at the Smuck Cemetery in the city of Bayham, Ontario. His headstone reads, "In memory of JOHN, beloved husband of Lusindia Boyce who died Aug. 24, 1854, aged 32 years."

Lusindia soon remarried, and the 1861 Canadian census lists her as the wife of Charles E. Arn (also printed as Orn and Orne), with her sons aged twelve, ten and eight. Lusindia and Charles, who was born in Germany and was four to five years younger than his wife, had several more children while living in Elgin County, according to the 1871 census: Sarah Almira (eleven), Watts E. (nine), Wilhelmina S. (also noted as Selina, six), Louisa (four), Charles Burt (two) and Truman F. (born in March of that year). A seventy-year-old Sarah Adams, Lusindia's mother, was also living with the family. The older sons would have all been adults and living on their own at this point.

The 1881 census notes the previously listed children, as well as fourteen-year-old Adell, born between Wilhelmina and Charles (perhaps a middle name for Louisa, given the matching age), while FindAGrave.com shows a Vineing W. Arn born in 1871. Vineing died the following year and thus did not appear on the 1891 census. Truman is also not noted in the 1881 documentation, so it is likely that he passed away sometime during the previous decade.

Tracking the life of William Boyce, the oldest son, has proven to be a bit of a challenge. Scouring census records via Ancestry.com and FamilySearch.org did lead to a couple of men with the same name, but they have far-fetched histories and are unlikely the correct man.

The younger son Chauncey married Hannah Lenora (Eastman or Eastmund) on April 10, 1874, in Highgate (Kent), Ontario. They eventually immigrated to the United States in 1877, when Chauncey was twenty-four. The couple had five children of their own: John Whitfield (1875–1952), Benjamin E. (1880–?), Oren Chauncey (1883–1939), Watts Pearl (1886–1921) and Harriett L. (1887–1982). The four youngest were born in Sanilac, in Michigan's "Thumb" region, where Chauncey lived and worked as a farmer.

By 1871, young John (with his last name spelled "Boice") was twenty years old, and according to the "Nominal Return of the Living," one of nine schedules under the Canadian census, was living in District No. 23 South Huron, Sub District Town of Goderich (on the eastern shore of Lake Huron, about seventy-five miles north of Sarnia), working as a cooper and building barrels that were used in shipping fish and other goods throughout the region.

Within a few years, John made his way to America, crossing two Great Lakes (Lake Huron and Lake Michigan) to land in Door County, Wisconsin. It wasn't long before he was considered a Pilot "Islander," with his name first appearing in 1874, as noted in *Washington Island: 1836–1876*, written in 1980 by Conan Bryant Eaton (70–71):

"The extent of pound net fishing at the time is suggested by the number of islanders who appeared before the justice of the peace to file 'fishing claims,' which were then registered in the courthouse exactly as were deeds to land. Typically, the fishermen 'inscribed' their names on 'monuments' of timber, which they erected near the beach 'for the purpose of claiming the water outside in Green Bay for fishing with a pound net.' Filing in 1874 were: John M. Boyce, S. Gunderson and B. Lind; Anderson Irr and Ferdinand LaBack; Patrick O'Neill and Loyal Baker, and Hugh O'Neill, who used the schoolhouse on the beach as a bearing in describing the location."

John apparently settled into island life well and was mentioned on occasion in the local newspapers for participating in a variety of community activities. They even referred to him as "Brother Boyce," a moniker that was readily used when writing about the young man. The March 7, 1878 issue of the *Door County Advocate* shed light on his social side, as the writer mentioned him in the updates from Washington Harbor: "We had the usual 'shin dig' on the 22[d]. Messrs, Little and Sanford furnished the music, and Brother John Boyce the crackers and cheese and the 'cup that cheers but not inebriates.' And the young people had an enjoyable time." Later accounts reference one of Boyce's favorite pastimes. "Brother Boyce is heavy in the rabbit business, and if they keep on increasing, he will soon have his hands full" was the report from Washington Harbor in the July 10, 1879 *Door County Advocate.*

But it wasn't all fun and games where John was concerned. He proved himself a hearty soul when it came to weathering the winters of northeastern Wisconsin and the often-dangerous shoreline of one of the largest freshwater lakes in the world.

A harrowing winter tale emerged in February 1879, as noted in several articles that appeared in the *Door County Advocate.* The February 20 issue shared an account written by William C. Betts, the lighthouse keeper on nearby Rock Island. Apparently, Betts and two other men (including John Boyce) attempted to cross the waters surrounding the Door County Peninsula in late January of that year. The colorful, entertaining and detailed account reads as follows (broken into paragraph form by this author for ease of reading):

> *I will attempt to tell you about our trip across the "Door" on our way home on the 26th of January last. At Elison* [sic] *Bay, we found the ice broken up so that it was impossible to cross that way, and after trying three times to go out on the ice, I gave it up and concluded to go in a boat, provided that we could get one large enough to carry our pony and three men.*
>
> *Brother Boyce, who wanted to get home as much as I did, went over to Europe Bay and got the loan of a large pound boat, putting in our horse and started. (Mistake No. 1.) The night had been quite still, so that the lake was frozen as far as we could see, the new ice being almost half an inch thick. My intention at starting was to go to the southward of Pilot Island and land on the east side of Detroit Island; or, if the water was clear of ice, to go right to Washington Island; but as we pushed off from the land, the wind began to blow fresh from the southward, and the weather looked so bad that we pointed our "clipper" for Plum Island. (Mistake No. 2.)*
>
> *We got along swimmingly until we got about three-quarters of a mile off Plum Island, when we discovered that there was ice all around the island, and we could not pass either the east or west end, and there was ice along the south shore so that it was doubtful if we could land; the wind by this time was blowing half a gale from the south, and our horse began to get queasy or seasick, and after a short consultation, we determined to work through the ice to the island, get on shore, wait 'till the ice passed and then go on to Detroit Harbor. (Mistake No. 3.)*
>
> *We got into the ice so far that we could not get out, the wind and sea increasing all the time; but we kept on pushing for the shore 'till at last we came to ice about a foot thick in large cakes close together and not moving at all, and then Brother Boyce commenced using the italic language with a vim. To go back now was impossible, and to go ahead with the boat was also out of the question. We held a "council of war," and I went ashore on the cakes, jumping from one to another, and while on shore, concluded to try and get the pony out of the boat and see if we could land him.*
>
> *Having cut some switches to encourage him with, I went back, and Brother B. took the halter and started for shore, and I after him, and*

when the pony came to a crack or opening between the ice cakes I would hit him a whack, and in this way, we got ashore in a short time. The ice was now moving up and [illegible] *at a lively rate, caused by the heavy sea running in from the lake. Here, we made mistake No. 4, for we had a harness and should have hitched the horse to the boat and hauled it up to the shore, but we did not think we could get the horse over the ice without his getting in two or three times, and we did not then think we should have to abandon the boat, for we expected the wind would cause an opening to be made somewhere.*

About this time, the italic language of Brother Boyce began to have some effect on the atmosphere, and the wind increased to a gale, the ice began to move slowly toward the northwest, gradually carrying the boat further from land, the heavy sea making it difficult to stand on the ice. But Capt. Peterson and Brother B. would not leave the boat 'till it was evident that to stay longer would be very dangerous, so they gave it up and came ashore. There we were, all tired and wet, with no ax and little or nothing to eat. By good fortune, I had two or three matches, with which we built a fire, and we also had some fresh pork, which we roasted. Here, we spent the long night. Capt. Peterson never camped out before. He was almost sick at Elison [sic] *Bay before we started but never uttered a word of complaint.*

At eleven o'clock that night, the wind changed to the northwest, which brought the ice back by daylight. I saw that the ice extended to Washington Island, so I called my companions and told them that I would make the at [sic] *attempt to reach that island. I started on foot, leaving the pony and everything on Plum Island. I crossed on the drifting ice and did not lose much of my valuable time until I set foot on Washington Island, where I met two Icelandic friends, who saw our fire the night before and were on the lookout for us.*

Brother B. and the Captain had waited on Plum Island to see if I could succeed in getting across, and when they saw me land safely, the former shouldered his box of lame rabbits (which a handsome young lady at Sturgeon Bay had made him a present of), and the two came over all right shortly after I had landed. I imagined I heard a wagon somewhere, but on rounding a point of land, I met a party of men with a boat, every one of them having either a basket, bucket or half barrel of provisions in their possession. They had seen our fire and were a party going to the rescue. Among the party were Messrs, Rohn, P. Flanigan, and some gentlemen from Sheboygan, whose acquaintance I then made for the first time.

I got home to Rock Island that same day, but Brother Boyce went back to Plum Island for the pony and some "traps" that we had left there and got caught by the running ice and had to stay another night. He had three good boys along to keep him out of mischief, who led the horse across the ice to Washington Island. I am happy to say that we are all doing well, including horse, rabbits, etc., but I don't want any more crossing the "Door" in a boat with a horse for shipmate in mine.

The following February, John faced similar accounts when trying to cross the dangerous waters in what was described as "simply abominable this winter." On February 5, the *Door County Advocate* noted: "John Boyce and Geo. Furlong crossed the 'Door' in an open boat the 20th inst. J.N. Cornell, assistant keeper of Poverty Island lighthouse, has been trying to cross for the last four or five weeks, but has not succeeded up to date. Jesse Minor crossed the dangerous passage two weeks ago on which occasion the ice was so thin that he could drive his sounding-pole through it at every step. None dare venture but our worthy Minor, who is determined to obey orders of the P.O. department no matter what the obstacles or impediments."

Certainly, surviving such ordeals not only made for good stories about town, but they likely reinforced John's ability to tackle dangerous situations and solve problems—key attributes for, let's say, a lighthouse keeper. That fall, John found himself in a new occupation, one he would have for the rest of his short-lived life. "Brother Boyce will report for duty on Oct. 1 as assistant keeper at the Pilot Island light-house [*sic*], in place of Mr. Byron Olson, resigned," said an October 9, 1879 brief in the *Door County Advocate.* "John will take his rabbits with him."

Among his duties at that time of year would have been preparing the lighthouse for the winter season. Typically, in the Great Lakes region, commercial activity slows toward the end of the year, given the ice buildup on the water, and it remains inactive until the spring thaw. The "Monthly Weather Review," published by the Washington Weather Bureau, noted that service closed around November 30, 1879, and resumed on April 1, 1880. A long, cold and snowy winter awaited John Boyce and his nest of rabbits.

The work returned with the changing of the seasons, yet John—a quirky sort of fellow—never really took to his role as assistant light keeper.

In the 1948 booklet *A Gleam Across the Wave: The Biography of Martin Nicolai Knudsen, Lighthouse Keeper on Lake Michigan*, lighthouse keeper/author Martin Knudsen and his son Arthur Knudsen share some history about John Boyce

The 1883 view of Pilot Island Lighthouse in Door County, Wisconsin. *Courtesy of the National Archives.*

(2006, 49–50) from the spring and early summer of 1880. During this period, Martin Knudsen was serving as the local justice of the peace.

"Every penny was important now that Martin [Knudsen] had four mouths to feed, and Theresa [Wilhelmine (Koyen) his wife] helped out whenever she could by knitting warm woolen mittens, socks and caps. One of her customers was John Boyce, assistant keeper of the light at Pilot Island and an excellent carpenter during the off seasons. John Boyce was an eccentric bachelor who was continually surprising the community by his strange conduct. He was a spiritualist and sometimes spent the night in the cemetery or sitting quietly on the church steps. He seemed to be strangely affected by the different phases of the moon, and on one occasion while assistant at Pilot Island lighthouse, he took the sailboat belonging to the lighthouse and irresponsibly sailed away to Escanaba, Michigan [about thirty miles], leaving the keeper alone and depriving him of his one means of communication with Washington Island or the mainland for almost two weeks.

"One spring day, John Boyce made mention of the fact to Martin Knudsen that he thought he would be 'leaving Pilot Island lighthouse before very long.' At home, when Martin told Theresa about this remark of John Boyce's, she wanted him to sit down immediately and write an application to Captain Davison for the assistant keeper's position in case John Boyce left. Martin hesitated to apply for another man's job, but on the other hand, John

Boyce had made no secret of the matter, and after a few days of thinking it over, he wrote the application and was on his way to the post office to mail it when he again met John Boyce on the road. Martin told him about the letter, and John Boyce offered to take it out to Captain Davidson for him."

Less than a year into his service, Boyce apparently fell victim to a state of depression; it was perhaps related to his work but was more likely due to the fact that his heart had recently been broken by a local woman who ended their relationship. On June 20, 1880, just ten days after logging his name in the federal census as a boarder and assistant to lighthouse keeper Emanuel Davidson (and interestingly, two days before a full moon), a distraught twenty-nine-year-old Boyce took his own life in a brutal and violent way. The *Green Bay Advocate*, on July 1, 1880, published "Suicide—It is reported here that John M. Boyce, assistant light-keeper at Pilot Island, committed suicide last week by cutting his throat with a razor, while insane."

The July 1, 1880 edition of the *Door County Advocate* featured a more detailed account:

> *I wish I could write you a cheerful letter, but alas, this time, it cannot be. An event has just happened that makes me, and indeed all of us, feel sad.*
>
> *Our young friend John M. Boyce is no more, his place is vacant. Yesterday, at Pilot Island, he terminated his earthly existence by cutting his throat. He has, for several weeks past, been in quite a low way, and his friends vainly tried to cheer him up. I saw him on Tuesday, the 15th. We all felt sorry to see him looking so sad and care-worn. He absolutely looked ten years older, but he would not say what the trouble was.*
>
> *Yesterday, he complained to Captain and Mrs. Davidson that he felt unwell and refused his dinner. He went out apparently to take a walk on the beach after dinner. The workmen who are fixing the new fog signal took a stroll in search of duck eggs and found poor John laid in the bushes, quite dead. His throat had three deep gashes in it, one on the right and two on the left side. Any one of the cuts would have been fatal. Today, an inquest was held, and this evening, all that remains of John M. Boyce was committed to the earth.*
>
> *He had many fine qualities and a true generous heart. He was esteemed by all and had not a single enemy. Peace be to his ashes. Would that his departure had been otherwise.*
>
> *Mr. Martin Knudsen will probably fill the vacancy as assistant light-keeper—a very good appointment, I believe.*

June 20 1880.

1st. Assistant Mr. John Boyce wentinto the bushes and commited
suceide. by cutting his throat with a razor at about 1:PM
some of Mr. Millers work men who were doing some building for
our fog signal, happened to walk around the beach, discouvered
Mr. Boyce laying down on his face, and called to him, but there was
no answer, then they walked up and seen blood on his hands, they called
me and we turned him over but he was dead, we seen that he had two
deep gashes, one on each side of the throat. Mr Miller the foreman
had his men build a coffin and took the beady body to Wash. Is.
and heald a furneral, this was a sad day out here and also in Detroit
harbor, The men returned to this station the next-day.

Signed Davison.
Keeper.

Lighthouse keeper Emanuel Davison makes a notation about the suicide of his assistant keeper, John Boyce, in his logbook. *Courtesy of the Washington Island Archives.*

The official record of the situation came from Keeper Davison, who noted in his log on June 19, 1880, that "1st. Assistant Mr. John Boyce does not feel well." The following day he reported the grisly details: "1st. Assistant Mr. John Boyce went into the bushes and commited [*sic*] suceide [*sic*], by cutting his throat with a razor at about 1 PM. Some of Mr. Millers work men who were doing some building for our fog signal happened to walk around the beach, discouvered [*sic*] Mr. Boyce laying down on his face and called to him, but there was no answer, then they walked up and seen blood on his hands, they called me, and we turned him over, but he was dead, we seen that he had two deep gashes, one on each side of the throat. Mr. Miller, the foreman, had his men build a coffin and took the body to Wash. Is. and heald [*sic*] a funeral, this was a sad day out there and also in Detroit Harbor, the men returned to this station the next day."

The person who was called out to Pilot Island to investigate Boyce's death was the local justice of the peace, none other than Martin Knudsen, who arrived "with a selected jury to preside at the inquest into the death of John Boyce by what was undoubtedly suicide."

Knudsen's book shares more details about the situation that fateful Sunday: "During the inquest, it developed that John Boyce had helped Norwegian Mads Hansen butcher a cow that week and that he had been particularly curious and interested about the location of the jugular vein. Sunday, John Boyce had refused to eat his dinner, and keeper Davidson saw him start off on a walk toward the north end of the island. Being used to his moods, the Davidsons took no unusual notice of his actions, but in the afternoon, Captain Davidson and the mason took a walk around the island and came upon the body of John Boyce lying face down on some boards, neatly arranged in a manner to keep the blood from his clothes. He had cut his jugular vein."

Following John's death, his younger brother, Chauncey, arrived from Michigan to settle his affairs. John Marvin Boyce was then buried in the old section of Island Cemetery in Washington (section 01-24). No headstone remains, and while there are others buried nearby with the Boyce name, they do not appear to be family members of the former assistant keeper.

Chauncey Boyce died of kidney disease on July 16, 1912, at the age of just fifty-nine, and Hannah died of pneumonia on April 5, 1931, at the age of eighty-one. They were both buried in the Clam Lake Township Cemetery in Wexford County, Michigan. Several descendants of the extended family remain in this area.

Lusindia Adams Boyce Arn died on June 5, 1885, at the age of fifty-five in Elgin County, Ontario, and was buried at the Straffordsville Cemetery. Her second husband, Charles, died of pneumonia on January 13, 1905, at the age of seventy-two and was buried beside her. There is little record of the children they had together. There is also no indication of when William Amos died or where he is buried.

Emanuel and Christine Davidson were transferred to the Grand Haven South Pierhead Range Light, serving from 1883 until 1900. In all, they accumulated almost twenty-four years of lighthouse service, fifty-nine years

John Boyce was buried in the old section (01-24) of the Washington Island Cemetery following his June 1880 suicide. No marker remains. *Courtesy of the Washington Island Archives.*

Pilot Island and its abandoned lighthouse sit on a remote and desolate island, reflective of something from an Alfred Hitchcock movie. *Author's collection.*

of marriage, four children (two boys and two girls) and more than twenty grandchildren and great-grandchildren. Emanuel died at the age of eighty-eight on March 28, 1911, in Sturgeon Bay (on the Door County Peninsula), Wisconsin; Christine died on January 7, 1922, at the age of eighty-nine. Both were buried in Bayside Cemetery in Sturgeon Bay.

Martin Knudsen was appointed to fill John Boyce's vacancy as assistant lighthouse keeper at Pilot Island. He served just two years there before transferring to the South Manitou Island Lighthouse in Lake Michigan in 1882. He would make his way back to Pilot Island in the fall of 1889, serving until there 1897, when he took an appointment at nearby Plum Island (1897–99). From there, he served an eighteen-year stint at the Racine Harbor Light (1899–1917), followed by seven years at the Milwaukee North Pier Lighthouse, where he retired in 1924 after forty-four years of service at Lake Michigan lights. Theresa died on September 24, 1933, at the age of seventy-eight, followed by Martin in 1943 at the age of about eighty-eight. They were buried in the Graceland Cemetery in Racine, Wisconsin.

In 1962, the Pilot Island Lighthouse was automated (the same year the fog signal was removed) and is one of ten historic beacons in Door County; it was listed in the National Register of Historic Places in 1972. The island and lighthouse are currently owned and managed by the United States Fish and Wildlife Service as part of the Green Bay National Wildlife Refuge, which also includes Hog Island, Plum Island, St. Martin Island and Rock Island (and soon to include Poverty Island Lighthouse) and is designated as a sanctuary for colonial nesting birds. The grounds, dwelling and tower on Pilot Island are all closed to all public entry.

The Pilot Island Lighthouse remains an active aid to navigation and is viewable from the Washington Island Ferry as well as private boat charters that take passengers out past the islands and historic lights of Door County. Plum Island is accessible during daylight hours from Memorial Day weekend through Labor Day weekend. Visitors will find four trails, as well as several maritime structures, including the Life Saving Station, 1849 lighthouse ruins, front and rear range lights, keeper's quarters and the fog signal building.

The Friends of the Plum and Pilot Islands (PlumAndPilot.org) a 501(c)(3) nonprofit, works with the FWS to "support the goals of preservation, restoration, maintenance and contemporary use of the lighthouses, accessories buildings and structures and other historic resources on Plum and Pilot Islands and to conserve and protect wildlife resources, while providing opportunities for quality wildlife-dependent recreation."

8

GROSSE POINT LIGHTHOUSE

EVANSTON, ILLINOIS

George Henry Sheridan was destined to become a lighthouse keeper. It was in his family's blood. In fact, ten members of the Sheridan and Moore (his mother's maiden name) families served at six different Lake Michigan lights between 1866 and 1940.

Born on October 18, 1868, on South Manitou Island in northern Lake Michigan (about ten miles west of Glen Arbor in today's Sleeping Bear Dunes National Lakeshore), George was the second of six sons of Aaron and Julia (Moore) Sheridan. According to the National Park Service's website (NPS.gov/slbe): "Aaron and his father, James, his uncle William and cousins Lyman and Newton Sheridan came from Oswego County in upstate New York to the Traverse City area about 1860. The Civil War called him [Aaron] into service of his country. In 1863, he was seriously wounded, losing the full use of his left arm. In 1865, he married Julia Moore, who was from the Chicago area, near where he had been hospitalized and recovered from the war wounds. Aaron had no previous lighthouse experience, but with a determined character and a courageous war record, he was selected for the South Manitou Island keeper job."

On July 21, 1866, the same year their oldest son, Levi, was born, Aaron and Julia moved into the lighthouse. Five other sons would follow: George, 1868; James, 1870; Alfred, 1872; Charles, 1875; and Robert, 1877. Midway through their service, in 1872, Julia was even appointed as an official assistant keeper, aiding Aaron in one of the most important lights in the region. She was one of about fifty women to serve in such a capacity in Michigan.

George Sheridan during his time of service at the Kalamazoo River Lighthouse in Saugatuck, Michigan. *Courtesy of Jack Sheridan.*

Tragedy struck the Sheridan family on March 15, 1878. Aaron, Julia and their nine-month-old son, Robert, were traveling back from the mainland in a small sailboat manned by an island fisherman named Christen Ancharson (also noted as Christen Anchersen Kragelund) when a storm blew in and capsized the boat. All three members of the Sheridan family perished that day—while sons Levi and George witnessed the accident from the lighthouse tower. The detailed story of this family's tragic history can be found in chapter 3 of *Michigan's Haunted Lighthouses.*

Lyman Sheridan (Aaron's first cousin) became the next family member to tend the South Manitou Island Light, serving from 1878 until 1888 with his wife, Mary, and their four children. That same year, Aaron and Julia's third son, Alfred (known as Alf), served a brief one-year stint at the Grosse Point Lighthouse in Evanston, Illinois, under Julia's brother Edwin J. Moore, who remained in the head keeper position until his death in 1924.

Despite the tragedy that struck the Sheridans on South Manitou Island, George felt a calling to become a lighthouse keeper to uphold the family legacy, even though what was lost all those years ago weighed heavily on him for the rest of his life. He began his lighthouse service as a third assistant keeper at the Chicago Harbor Lighthouse (1896–99) before moving along to the Calumet Harbor Lighthouse near Chicago as an assistant (1899–1905) and first assistant at the Michigan City East Pierhead Lighthouse (1905–09), with annual pay of $500, $450 and $540, respectively.

In 1909, he was hired as the only officially trained lighthouse keeper at the Kalamazoo River Light Station in Saugatuck (no longer standing), where he lived with his wife, Sarah (Unwin), and their three children: Joseph, James and George. His beginning salary was $552 a year.

Life for George had always been a struggle, given that he was about ten years old when his parents died off the coast of South Manitou Island. He and his brothers (aged between three and twelve) were sent to live in Bristol Village, Illinois, to be raised by their maternal grandparents, Henry and Julie Moore, without any additional financial assistance from the U.S. Lighthouse Service. There was no such thing as a pension or life insurance payout for descendants, although Julia Sheridan's brother Edwin Moore worked for years to change that.

The July 1, 1914 issue of the *Arizona Republic* provided details on the important Hamlin Bill that Moore was diligently advocating for, especially given the various tragedies his extended family had suffered during their years of service as government-appointed lighthouse keepers:

> *The Hamlin Bill, pending in the house of representatives, provides that all employees in the classified civil service of the United States shall be eligible for retirement on the following pensions: for thirty years or more of service, 60 percent of the average salary for the last five years; for twenty-five to thirty years, 45 percent; for twenty to twenty-five years, 40 percent. An employee who has served the United States for five years and who has been disabled without fault on his part shall receive 30 percent, for from five to ten years' service; 40 percent, for ten to twenty years; and 50 per cent for twenty years and over. All employees are to retire at the age of seventy years.*
>
> *These pensions are entirely independent of any contribution or savings by the employee. They are intended mainly to relieve the employee whose salary would not permit him to lay aside any material provisions for old age or disability; though under the terms of the bill those receiving high salaries will obtain benefits greater in amount than those receiving pay too low to provide for retirement.*

Possibly this and other features may require amendment in details. But there is no doubt that the vast body of mail carriers, clerks, and government employees work faithfully and at low salaries. Great corporations are generally providing for the pensioning of their aged employees, and the government should not be more neglectful of this duty than the corporations.

Among the supporters of this bill was Edward F. Kelley, a Democratic congressional candidate in 1914 from Detroit who stated in a July 12, 1914 *Detroit Free Press* article: "I am strongly in favor of the Hamlin Bill, now pending before the house of representatives, which provides for the retirement on pension of superannuated employees of the federal government, and contains a similar clause for men permanently disabled in the service."

That same year, news came that the lighthouse in Saugatuck was being decommissioned and that George and his family would need to relocate once again, this time to St. Joseph to the south, where a set of pier lights were built in 1906–07. This port was also home to the Lake Michigan Lighthouse Depot, which provided warehousing for supplies for all the lights on the southern part of that lake until a new facility was built and service was transferred to Milwaukee in 1917.

Yet before George could button up the Saugatuck Light and make the transition to St. Joe, he suffered a nervous breakdown. He checked himself into the Michigan State Hospital in Kalamazoo that October to seek treatment for his lifelong depression. From there, he appeared to have ultimately been transferred to the Lake Shore Sanitarium in Evanston (north of Chicago).

Back in Saugatuck, Sarah (George's wife) was appointed a temporary keeper, helping finalize details to close up the light and collect George's salary. She eventually found a home in town and took in laundry to make ends meet. By January 1, 1915, the U.S. Lighthouse Service stopped George's pay, and Sarah was left in further distress, accepting donations from other lighthouse keepers in the area to help cover her bills and raise her boys (aged four, six and nine). Life after service was tough on keepers and their families, as no pension, disability or retirement plans were yet available to assist them.

The February 27, 1915 issue of *St. Joseph Saturday Herald* shed light on the emotional and financial hardship that George and his family were facing under the headline "Lighthouse Keeper Fired from Service—George Sheridan Left Penniless After Relatives are Lost in Service":

> *Edwin Moore, for thirty-one years keeper of the Gross* [sic] *Point Lighthouse near Chicago, who is agitating the passage of the Hamlin Bill for the pensioning of lighthouse keepers, now before congress, Saturday, found an object lesson in treatment of lighthouse men in George Sheridan* [Edwin's nephew], *who is ill in the Lake Shore sanitarium, near Chicago.*
>
> *Sheridan has had a double dose of hard luck. In 1878, his father and mother and infant brother were lost from a boat while en route to the mainland from South Manitou Island, where the elder Sheridan was light keeper. George and four other children, all under 12 years of age, were left dependents.*
>
> *When George was old enough, he entered the lighthouse service and served for twenty years. In 1912* [actually 1909], *he was appointed keeper of the light at Saugatuck, Mich. The lighthouse was in bad repair, and he repaired it at his own expense.*
>
> *Last October, he succumbed to a nervous breakdown. The government stopped his pay Jan. 1. Lighthouse men are taking up a collection for Sheridan.*
>
> *Mr. Sheridan was to have been appointed to take the place of Roy Scott, who was transferred from St. Joseph to Milwaukee, but ill health prevented the appointment.*

On Tuesday, March 23, nearly five months after being institutionalized, George was released from the asylum as a "cured" man, and he went to visit his uncle Edwin Moore at Grosse Point Light, just a half mile away, for additional respite. The Grosse Point Lighthouse was built in 1873, and Moore served thirty-eight years there (all but two as the head keeper). Sadly, in the days that followed George's arrival, the Sheridan family's history took another dark turn.

The Saturday, March 27, 1915 issue of *Detroit Free Press* featured the news: "Michigan Lightkeeper Ends Life of Tragedy—George Sheridan of Unfortunate Family, Found Hanging in Shed at Evanston, Ill": "A life filled with misfortune came to a tragic end Tuesday, when George Sheridan, formerly of the government lighthouse at Saugatuck, Mich., and in the lighthouse service for 20 years, committed suicide by hanging in a little shed near the Grosse Pointe [*sic*] Lighthouse at North Evanston. His body was found today. Sheridan's father was a lighthouse keeper for 21 years. He and George's mother and an infant son were drowned when George was a boy. Two other brothers were drowned there at another time, and

The Grosse Point Lighthouse in Evanston, Illinois, around the time of George Sheridan's suicide there in 1915. *Courtesy of the Library of Congress.*

another was killed while working on a steel bridge. Sheridan leaves a wife and three little children."

A Chicago-area newspaper included more details about Sheridan's death under the headline "'HARD LUCK LIFE' ENDED BY ROPE IN LAKE SHACK": "Nothing more was seen of him until yesterday, when his body was found in the shack by Ernest Altenberg, a fisherman. He was lying on the ground, the rope he had tied around his neck having snapped from the weight of his body.

"The body was identified by Moore, who told the police Sheridan was not at home Tuesday morning and that none of the members of his family knew whether he had called.

"A wife and three little children survive my nephew. They are left without means of support, and their case presents another argument for government employees who have given the best years of their life in service to their country."

BURIED AT MT. HOPE CHICAGO

George H. Sheridan, lightkeeper at our harbor for the past six years, was buried at Mt. Hope Cemetery, Chicago on Sunday March 28th 1915.

The funeral was by automobiles and took place from the residence of his wife's sister in Chicago. Rev. H. I. Parrott of The Windsor Park Congregational Church officiating. Members of Niagara Lodge No. 141 K. of P. acted as pallbearers. Mr. Sheridan being a member of that lodge for the past twenty years.

Mr. Sheridan was born at the Lighthouse at South Manitou Island, Mich in 1868, and leaves to mourn his death his wife, three sons, Joseph, James and George and three brothers, Charles, of Newago Mich., Edward of Chicago and Alfred of Oregon.

Mr. Sheridan met death by hanging himself in a shed near the Gross Point light house in Illinois, after having received word from the Government that his services would be no longer required.

A front-page obituary for George H. Sheridan. *From the* Commercial Record *(Saugatuck).*

Following George's death, Lewis M. Stoddard, inspector for the Twelfth District, wrote, "Mr. Sheridan was considered one of the best and most trustworthy employees in the lighthouse service, and this office deeply regrets his loss."

George Sheridan was forty-six years old at the time of his death. He was buried on Sunday, March 28, at the Mt. Hope Cemetery in Chicago.

A few years after George's suicide, on June 20, 1918, Congress finally passed a bill providing retirement and disability for keepers—the first civil service to gain such benefits. The "Civil-Service Regulations for the Lighthouse Service" report of 1928 published the Lighthouse Service Retirement Act: "All officers and employees engaged in the field service or on vessels of the Lighthouse Service, except persons continuously employed in the district offices or shops and persons whose duties do not require substantially all their time, are included in the Lighthouse Service Retirement Act of June 20, 1918 (40 Stat. 608), which provides for optional retirement for persons who have reached the age of 65 years, after having been 30 years in the active service of the government and for compulsory retirement of persons who have reached the age of 70 years, regardless of length of service. The retired pay under this act shall be based on the average annual pay received for the last five years of active service and shall be one-fortieth of such average annual pay for each year of service, with a maximum of thirty-fortieths."

Sarah Sheridan lived to the age of eighty-eight, passing away of cardiovascular disease on April 3, 1967. She was buried at Riverside Cemetery in Saugatuck. Well known in town, Sarah was active in the Ladies' Aid Society of the Congregational Church and the Order of Eastern Star. It is said that her greatest joy in her later years, aside from being a grandmother, was to watch the goings-on of the village from the rocking chair of her home, which still stands and is now a retail shop in the boutique art community.

Several members of the Sheridan family remain in Allegan County, particularly in the Saugatuck-Douglas area, near the site where George and Sarah once served as keepers. Jack Sheridan, the son of their middle child, James, has been active for years with the Saugatuck-Douglas Historical Society. His younger brother, Stephen, served for seventeen years as a judge in Allegan County's Fifty-Seventh District Court before retiring in 2008.

PART V.

LAKE SUPERIOR

9

GRAND ISLAND LIGHTHOUSE

MUNISING, MICHIGAN

Much has been written about the tragic and gruesome deaths of two keepers at the Grand Island North Lighthouse near Munising in 1908. Even more has been speculated about the situation. Yet in the end, what really happened to them that summer will likely never be known.

Located in the heart of the Pictured Rocks National Lakeshore (established in 1966), the 13,500-acre Grand Island (eight miles long by four miles wide) is the largest island on Lake Superior's south shore. It was first home to a community of Chippewa Natives who hunted in the dense forests, foraged in the woodlands, paddled the rocky shoreline and fished the fresh waters. They called this area *Minnising*, meaning "place of the great island."

Voyageurs, missionaries, surveyors and fur traders, including John Jacob Astor and his American Fur Company, arrived next, setting up shop and bartering with the Natives. This occurred during the early 1840s, before the first permanent White settlers arrived on the island and when Abraham and Anna Marie (VanDyke) Williams made the trip from Decatur, Illinois, with their ten children. Today, Williams Landing, an unincorporated community in Murray Bay on Grand Island, is named for these early residents.

The first wooden lighthouse on the north end of Grand Island was constructed for $5,000 in 1856, just one year after the Soo Locks were completed in nearby Sault Ste. Marie, opening up Lake Superior's shipping routes. Reuben Smith was appointed the first keeper, serving until 1860. That same year, an intricate step-and-ladder system was built on the cliffs to provide access between the lighthouse and the lake below.

In 1860, an intricate step-and-ladder system was built on the cliffs to provide access between the Grand Island North Lighthouse and the lake below. *Courtesy of the U.S. Lighthouse Society.*

Three other keepers lived and worked in the original building, including William Chambers (1860–1861), George Wagner (1861–1865) and Reuben Frink (1867–1869), according to LighthouseFriends.com. Frink was the last keeper in that deteriorating structure and the first keeper in the new brick lighthouse, with its forty-foot-tall tower and fourth-order Fresnel lens, which was completed in 1867 at a cost of $17,000.

Years later, a tram system was added to the cliffside stairway, which traversed nearly 230 feet down to the boathouse and was located nearly a half mile southeast of the light. The website LighthouseFriends.com notes that the boathouse "was accessed by a trail that crossed four deep ravines spanned by bridges that had lengths of twenty-five, seventy, sixty-nine and forty-five feet. A boat landing, made of logs from the island and filled with stone, was built in 1902."

One of the noted keepers of this remote light was George Genry (also printed Genery). He served at just two lighthouses during his twenty-one-year career, including six years as the first assistant to John H. Malone at the

Isle Royale Menagerie Lighthouse (1887–93), where his starting salary was $400 annually. Genry was transferred to the Grand Island North Lighthouse in August 1893, and with the promotion came an increase in pay of $200 a year to support his wife, Johanna, and their large family (with children ranging in age from six months to thirteen years).

Toward the end of the nineteenth century, the Cleveland-Cliffs Iron Company was formed (the merging of the Cleveland Iron Mining Company and the Iron Cliffs Company), with offices in Ishpeming, just sixty miles west of Grand Island. William Mather, the company president and a noted conservationist, bought most of Grand Island around 1904 and established a game preserve and hotel for the enjoyment of his family and friends. And while the powerful man was the envy of many, Mather did have at least one apparent nemesis: George Genry.

Decades later, Genry's own children recalled that Mather wanted to own the entire island, but the U.S. Coast Guard held two key properties: the forty-five-foot-tall Grand Island East Channel Lighthouse on the south end (built in 1868) and the North Lighthouse, where Genry tended the light. On occasion, when animals from Mather's preserve made their way to the lighthouse property, Genry was said to take it upon himself to shoot, kill and eat them, which further infuriated Mather.

Ironically, there were rumors that Genry himself was a difficult fellow to work for or with. A quick review of the list of assistant keepers who served with him over his fifteen years on Grand Island supports that theory. There were ten in all between 1893 and 1908, including Herbert W. Weeks (1893–97), James Bruce (1897–1900), Robert Allen (1901–02), Edward Clark (1902), Charles C. Vanastine (1902–04), William C. Marshall (1904–05), Albert J. Smith (1905), Joseph Metivier (1905–07), Edward Sommer (1907–08) and Edward S. Morrison (1908).

A native of Tecumseh, Michigan, in Lenawee County, Morrison was born in 1879 under the name Edgar S. Morrison, according to Michigan state records of birth, the son of Rechab (also recorded as Recob, Rackib, Richard or Robert) and Elizabeth "Eliza" Jane (Foster). It is unclear when his name was changed to Edward, but the 1880 census still shows him as Edgar S., along with siblings James R., Lucy K., Lillian or "Lillie" (who was later murdered by her husband in 1893 in Toledo at the age of twenty-two), Mary E., Fanny, Minnie and Thomas L. One brother, Edwin, lived only one year (1877–1878).

Morrison enlisted as a seaman with the United States Navy Reserve on December 22, 1899, and was sent to St. Louis for basic training. He served aboard the USS *Dixie*, a training ship for recruits that sailed to the West Indies, the Mediterranean, through the Suez Canal to the Philippines and, later, through the Caribbean and the Panama Canal Zone. He was discharged on December 21, 1903, and returned to his home at 11394 Martindale Avenue in Detroit.

A year later, Morrison moved to Flint, where he worked at the Imperial Wheel Works for three years and engaged in social activities as a member of the Friendship Lodge, IOOF (Order of Odd Fellows). While there, he also met and later married Lena A. Johnson, the daughter of Eugene and Cora (Hudson) Johnson, on August 17, 1905, in Essex, Ontario.

Morrison was hired in the spring of 1908 as Genry's assistant lighthouse keeper. In late April, he made the 350-mile trek north from Flint to Grand Island, starting in his position on Friday, May 1. It was his first (and last) position with the lighthouse service. Lena stayed home, expecting to meet up with her husband later in the summer, once he was settled in at his post. Sadly, she would never make it to Grand Island or see her beloved husband again.

By all accounts, it was known that Genry had taken one of the lighthouse sailboats to Munising on Saturday, June 6, 1908, to collect the monthly pay for himself and his assistant. Based on his annual salary listed with the United States Lighthouse Society Archives (archives.uslhs.org), this would have been $50 for himself and about $30 to $35 for Morrison, whose starting annual salary is noted as $400.

Locals also reported seeing Genry, alone, in town that morning, procuring groceries and other supplies, including a bottle of whiskey. A newspaper account in the *Daily Mining Journal* noted, "He had been drinking in town and was pretty well under the influence of liquor when he left" around 10:00 or 11:00 a.m. That meant he either got a pretty early start on the drinking or had been on a multiday bender, as a *Detroit Free Press* article noted "they also assert that he was drinking heavily all last week."

During the boat ride back to Grand Island, according to an account written by Munising historian and author Faye Swanberg, Genry "was sighted passing East Channel Light, then by fishermen in Trout Bay—the last to see the 48-year-old keeper alive."

This is when the timeline and stories begin to change, depending on the source. Some accounts say that a team of men from Munising ventured out to the island after noticing the light had been dark for several days. Others say it was the discovery of a body in a boat near the mainland that initiated an investigation. Either way, what the men found when they arrived at the

A sailboat similar to those that keepers would have used at the Grand Island North Lighthouse. *Courtesy of the Alger County Historical Society.*

lighthouse dock led to more questions than answers and ultimately gave life to a slew of theories about what happened to the two keepers.

Apparently, when Genry arrived back on the island, he unloaded the boat, one of two or maybe three assigned to the station, and the provisions were left stacked up on the dock. A wheelbarrow nearby indicated that either he or his assistant was preparing to transport these items back up the cliff to the lighthouse.

An empty whiskey bottle was spotted near the landing, leading to speculation that Genry had potentially polished off the liquor on his return trip. "Genry had a bad reputation, he drank, drank each time he came to town and [was] generally drunk when he left for the light," Swanberg noted. "When drinking, he was surly, combative." Genry's wife, however, adamantly denied that her husband ever drank to excess and claimed that the bottle had likely washed ashore after being tossed into Lake Superior by some other unknown individual.

Genry's jacket was also found hanging in the boathouse, and Morrison's vest was discovered draped over a kitchen chair inside the lighthouse, his watch and papers still in the pocket. Newspaper accounts also noted that Morrison had been reading up on lighthouse regulations while cooking dinner when Genry returned, and a pan of meat and potatoes was left on the stove, uneaten.

What wasn't found were either of the keepers (or their monthly pay). Two boats were also missing. In checking the logs, the last journal entry was dated Friday, June 5, and the slate entry for June 6 was in Morrison's handwriting. As a search for the men and details about their disappearances was underway, volunteers manned the light until the arrival of a temporary keeper, Joseph Prato, on Friday, June 12. That was also the day that a badly decomposed and, some say, mutilated body was found floating in one of the lighthouse boats near a beach some twenty-five miles east. A log entry from head keeper Irvine Thomas at the Au Sable Light Station on June 12 broke the first news of a body having been discovered.

"2^d Asst. [Emil Kohnert] ret. 9 A.M. Mr. Wm. Van Dusen of Grand Marias reported a lighthouse boat ashore with a dead man in her about 9 mile W. of Station. I sent 1st Asst. [Young Orrin] to report it to Life Saving Station. Crew arrived here 9 P.M. I went up with them and brought boat to station, they took body to Gd. Marais, man apparently died from exposure, as he was lying under the forward deck, foremast gone, mainmast standing boat was in good shape and only one small hole in her. I think it is from Grand Island Light Station."

At the onset, the identity of the body was not readily known, as reflected in the countless articles that appeared in newspapers around the country in the days and weeks that followed. The Monday, June 15, 1908 edition of the *Detroit Free Press* ran a front-page story (above the fold) with the headline "SLAIN AND SET AFLOAT":

> *Brutally murdered, then robbed and their mutilated bodies set afloat in open boats upon Lake Superior is believed to have been the fate of George Genry, keeper of the north light on Grand Island, and his assistant, whose name has not been learned.*
>
> *The body of Genry's assistant, with the head disfigured beyond recognition, was found in one of the lighthouse sailboats, which was picked up by the Au Sable Lifesaving Patrol yesterday between Munising and Grand Marais. This led to an investigation, and the further discovery was made that Keeper Genry was missing from his post.*

A Lighthouse Found Vacant.

> *Genry was in Munising June 6 after provisions and returned to the lighthouse intending to come to the city again yesterday to move his family to the lighthouse home. He failed to put in appearance, and the finding of the*

body of his assistant in the lighthouse boat caused the authorities to get into communication with Munising. The body was soon identified as that of Genry's new assistant, but no one knew his name. He having but recently arrived here to take up his new position.

Officers were at once dispatched to the Grand Island Light. They found it abandoned. The provisions were found in the boathouse near the light, but both of the keepers' boats were missing.

Not Lighted Thursday Night.

The lighthouse is located on the extreme north point of Grand Island, seven miles from the nearest habitation, the home of the keeper of the Cleveland Cliff Game Preserve. It is 16 miles from Munising, upon an isolated rocky coast. There is a report here that the light was not lighted Thursday night [five days], *but this has not been definitely confirmed.*

Intense excitement prevails here and at Grand Marais, and officers and searching parties are making every effort to find Genry, although little hope is entertained that the keeper will be found alive. Both Genry and his assistant are said to have received their pay the day Genry was here, June 6, and the fear is general that they were probably the victims of a planned robbery and murder.

The *Detroit Free Press* ran an equally long story the next day under the headline "DETROITER SLAIN NEAR LIGHTHOUSE. Mystery in Tragedy at Grand Island Deepens—Victim Is Identified as E.S. Morrison." In addition to the earlier mentioned claim that Genry had been drinking heavily, this article also states that a "Free Press representative found one man who is positive that he saw Mr. Gennery [*sic*] in Munising on Tuesday or Wednesday, June 9 or 10, and two men who will swear that they saw him here on Tuesday, June 9," thus fueling speculation about what really happened to Morrison earlier in the month.

In his book *Great Lakes Crime*, author and historian Fred Stonehouse also referred to apparent sightings of Genry at several Munising saloons after the date his assistant went missing—supporting claims that the keeper unleashed a wrath on Morrison that led to his death. "At some point, he realized the danger of his scheme and went home, where his wife hid him from the authorities until it was safe for him to flee town," Stonehouse wrote. "Where he ended up is unknown, but there are claims that he went to Canada and lived out his days in obscurity."

Another newspaper article, under the headline "KEEPER'S WIFE NOT WORRIED. Believed She Knows the Location of Missing Genry. She Says Husband Quarreled with Dead Detroit Man," reveals possible motive. The piece also noted, "It is believed that she is withholding information." Such theories would come to light again many years later.

Just a day or two after Morrison's body was identified—based on a tattoo with thirteen stars located on his left arm, according to Northern Michigan University's Center for U.P. Studies (as published on NMU.edu)—his wife, Lena, received a letter from him that revealed some shocking details:

"Do not be surprised if you hear of my body being found dead along the shore of Lake Superior," Morrison wrote, as noted in a newspaper article published on June 17. Morrison also wrote that "the keeper, Genry, was of a quarrelsome disposition and that he feared an assault if he opposed him. He said the former had never been able to keep an assistant more than one season."

Some stories that conveyed the belief that Morrison didn't know how to man a sailboat seem far-fetched, given that he served four years with the U.S. Navy Reserve and he clearly would have the skills necessary in normal weather conditions. In fact, this was a theory disputed by the Morrisons' friends in an article under the headline "AN EXPERT SAILOR. E.S. MORRISON ACCUSTOMED TO HANDLING SAILBOATS. Friend of Dead Assistant Lighthouse Keeper Tells of His Ability in that Direction":

"Morrison was an able seaman and perfectly familiar with boats of all kinds," said Mr. F.G. Menke [of Detroit] to the *Daily Journal*. "As a matter of fact, he had to demonstrate his knowledge in this respect before he could get the government job of assistant keeper at the north light on Grand Island. Morrison was the owner of a 232-foot sailboat on the Detroit River, and he had given repeated evidence of his skill in handing the craft under all sorts of conditions. He may have died from exposure, which I very much doubt, but his death was in no way due to an inability on his part to manage the sailboat in which his dead body was found."

Weather may or may not have played a contributing factor in the death of these lighthouse keepers. The June 16 *Detroit Free Press* article noted, "The prevailing winds were from the south so that a boat pushed off the shore at Sand Point, the nearest point on the mainland to Grand Island, would have drifted out to sea. Had the wind changed, the boat would have been driven upon pictured rocks and its contents never discovered until the sea gives up its dead."

The June 1908 reports from the U.S. Department of Agriculture, Weather Bureau (with observations out of Marquette) noted that the area temperatures during the first week of the month were above average. On Saturday, June 6, the day that Genry and Morrison disappeared, the temperatures ranged from 65 to 85 degrees Fahrenheit, with clear skies in the morning and cloudy conditions at 7:00 p.m. Thunderstorms were reported in the area on June 6–7, but nothing severe was documented. And while a cold front moved in around June 9, temperatures throughout the month remained above freezing—nothing too extreme on either end of the spectrum to cause death by exposure in the fresh waters of Lake Superior, unless Morrison's condition had been compromised in some way.

Edward S. Morrison served just weeks as a lighthouse keeper before his untimely death in June 1908. *From* Detroit Free Press, *June 1908.*

Medical professionals were stumped by the case, and with no real suspects, leads or criminal investigation, they seemed content with issuing a benign cause of death. Even after a second coroner's jury investigation and strong suspicions of murder or some other nefarious activity (given the severity of the injuries to his head and shoulders), Morrison's death certificate, signed by Dr. James Anderson, Grand Marais coroner, listed "exhaustion, result of exposure in an open boat in Lake Superior" as the cause of death.

The days following the discovery of Morrison's body were stressful for the family, who simply wanted to lay the man to rest. Apparently, with the two inquisitions into the cause of death, there was a delay in releasing Morrison's body for burial.

Messages were sent to officials in Munising, asking that the body be sent at once to Flint, where the local Odd Fellows Lodge planned to pay for services. Two days had passed without any communication from authorities, prompting Flint deputy sheriff Charles Raab to reach out on behalf of the family. One newspaper account indicated that the undertaker, William Wesley Bowerman of Bowerman Funeral Home, was demanding one hundred dollars before agreeing to send the body, which first went to Detroit before finally arriving in Flint.

The service was quite an affair, and the June 19, 1908 issue of the *Flint Journal* ran a notice that read: "Detroit young men who served in the United States Navy during the years from 1899 to 1903 have requested that if there are any former members of the navy in Flint, they attend the funeral of E.S. Morrison, the Flint man found dead in a sailboat off the shore of Lake Superior, near Munising. It is requested that Flint young men who were in the navy during the period referred to meet tonight at 706 Margaret Street to make plans for attending the funeral, which will be held as soon as possible after the arrival of the remains, which are en route to this city from Munising, according to the latest advices received by relatives of the deceased."

The funeral was held at the Methodist Protestant Church on North Saginaw Street in Flint, the pastor Rev. Milo J. Weaver officiating. Morrison's obituary states the service was "largely attended by friends and acquaintances, and the casket covered with a profusion of flowers, the service was one of the impressiveness. Among those present were members of Friendship Lodge of Odd Fellows, of which the deceased was a member. His final resting place is the Avondale Cemetery in Flint (Genesee County)."

Now, if Genry had gotten away with murdering Morrison and escaped out of the country as some say, how did that explain the finding of his own body a month after his assistant? A body so badly decomposed that identification was made based on the vest matching the one Genry was seen wearing while in Munising on June 6 as well as papers found in his pocket. Clearly, no forensic DNA testing was available at the time to prove conclusively that the remains were those of keeper Genry.

On Wednesday, July 8, 1908, the *Iron Port* out of Escanaba (Delta County) was the first paper to report that Genry's remains had been discovered.

"Word has been received of the finding of the remains of Keeper Genry, for many years in charge of the North Light on Grand Island, which were cast upon the beach some ten miles below Munising. This is the final chapter in a double tragedy. A month or so ago, Genry sailed from Munising in the lighthouse tender. It is believed that he persuaded Morrison, the assistant lightkeeper, whom he picked up at the light landing, to make a run out to some nets, to get fresh fish, and he fell overboard and was drowned. Morrison, who could not sail a boat, was blown hither and thither on the lake until he died of exposure. His remains were found by a lifesaving patrolman in the boat, which had finally been cast upon the beach by the wind. A verdict of death from exposure was returned by the coroner's jury. There has been a moral certainty on the part of those acquainted with the facts in the case that Genry was drowned, although at first it was reported that Morrison had been killed by him."

On Sunday, July 12, 1908, the *Detroit Free Press* ran a story under the headline "BODY OF GRAND ISLAND LIGHT KEEPER FOUND":

Right: Edward S. Morrison was buried in the Avondale Cemetery in Flint, Michigan (Genesee County). *Author's collection*.

Below: George Genry's certificate of death, signed by Dr. Theodore W. Scholtes, a well-respected local physician and coroner, indicated "accidental drowning" as the ultimate cause of his 1908 demise. *Courtesy of the State of Michigan.*

PLACE OF DEATH
County of Alger
Township of
or
Village of Munising
or
City of (No. St.; Ward)

STATE OF MICHIGAN
Department of State—Division of Vital Statistics
CERTIFICATE OF DEATH

144

13
Registered No. 12

[If death occurred in a Hospital or Institution, give its NAME instead of street and number. If away from usual residence, give "Special Information" below.]

FULL NAME George Genry

AUG 11 1908

PERSONAL AND STATISTICAL PARTICULARS

SEX Male
COLOR White
DATE OF BIRTH (Month) Jan (Day) 27 (Year) 1860
AGE 48 years, 4 months, 9 days
SINGLE, MARRIED, WIDOWED, OR DIVORCED Married
AGE AT MARRIAGE, NUMBER OF CHILDREN — If married, age at (first) marriage 34 years. Parent of 5 children, of whom 5 are living
BIRTHPLACE (State or country) Ontonogan Mich
NAME OF FATHER Eli Genry
BIRTHPLACE OF FATHER (State or country) Canada
MAIDEN NAME OF MOTHER Mary Jane Adams
BIRTHPLACE OF MOTHER (State or country) Canada
OCCUPATION Light House Keeper

THE ABOVE STATED PERSONAL PARTICULARS ARE TRUE TO THE BEST OF MY KNOWLEDGE AND BELIEF
(Informant) Mrs Jane Cadraut
(Address) Duluth Minn

MEDICAL CERTIFICATE OF DEATH

DATE OF DEATH (Month) June (Day) 6 (Year) 1908

I HEREBY CERTIFY, That I attended deceased from 190 , to , 190 , that I last saw h alive on 190 , and that death occurred, on the date stated above, at M.

The CAUSE OF DEATH was as follows:
Accidental Drowning
172 (DURATION) DAYS
Contributory (DURATION) DAYS

(Signed) TW Scholtes Coroner M. D.
July 13 1908 (Address) Munising

SPECIAL INFORMATION only for Hospitals, Institutions, Transients or Recent Residents:
Former or usual residence — How long at place of death? Days
Where was disease contracted, if not at place of death?

PLACE OF BURIAL OR REMOVAL Munising Mich
DATE OF BURIAL 7-13 1908
UNDERTAKER Wm H Bowerman
ADDRESS Munising Mich
Filed July 13, 1908 D. E. Simmons Registrar

With the discovery of the badly decomposed remains of Keeper George Genry, the mystery of the Grand Island lighthouse has been solved.

Nearly a month ago, Assistant Keeper Morrison, of Detroit, was found dead in a sailboat. Genry was missing and there were rumors of foul play, but it was decided by a coroner's jury that Morrison had perished from exposure. Today [July 11, per the dateline] *Genry's body was found in Lake Superior 20 miles from Munising. He had been drowned, but in what manner is unknown.*

R. C. McKenzie, of Munising, had gone to that locality near the pictured rocks, to see if the crop of blueberries was likely to be plentiful in that vicinity. Noticing a dark object upon the shore he put in close and found it to be the body of Genry. The coroner, with a jury, has gone out to view the remains and hold an inquest. The theory now generally held concerning the tragedy is that while intoxicated Genry fell overboard and was drowned, while Morrison was unable to handle the boat, died from exposure.

It should be noted that while wild blueberries do grow throughout the Upper Peninsula, particularly around the Lake Superior shoreline from Marquette to Whitefish Point, July 11 is quite early for picking. Typical harvesting takes place in mid-August to coincide with the Wild Blueberry Festival in Chippewa County, which runs annually during the third weekend of August.

No one was ever questioned or charged with robbery and/or murder of these two keepers, but there was speculation as to who might want to dispose of them.

In his 2002 book *Island of Adventure – Tales of Grand Island*, author Marc Weingart, who spent seventeen summers living on the island, shared comments passed down from Genry's children through Dr. Loren Graham, current owner of the lighthouse and author of *Death at the Lighthouse: A Grand Island Riddle*.

"He [Mather] really hated our father. He hired some professionals and told them: 'Get Genry, but don't tell me how you did it!' When George and Morrison first arrived at the lighthouse, they went inside, hung their coats on their hooks and put the groceries on the table. That was exactly how the Sheriff and his men had found the things. Mather's hired killers had probably already been inside North Light before the two keepers arrived. They had been hiding and waiting in the living room. They killed Morrison and George, put Morrison in the boat and got rid of George some other way. Perhaps they buried him somewhere on the island, or they simply threw him in the lake. Morrison's wounds came from the killing, but also from rolling around in the boat and banging his head in there."

There still are those who believe that Genry killed Morrison after a disagreement, set his bludgeoned body afloat and then made a quick stop home before fleeing to Canada, where he lived out his years in hiding until passing away in 1951. Despite the fact that Johanna Genry made a visit to the local sheriff in June 1908 requesting an inquisition after her husband failed to return home to collect the family for their summer on the island, some sources say she waited to apply for his pension (although such programs weren't available to lighthouse keepers until 1918).

Other locals recall another situation in 1951 which supports this storyline. Genry's daughter, also named Johanna, supposedly left her post as a teacher in Munising during the school year to travel with her family to Canada. No legitimate reason was given, but the timing could support theories that the keeper had turned fugitive in order to hide from authorities.

Genry, who was born in Ontonagon, Michigan, to Eli and Mary Jane (Adams) Genry on January 27, 1860 (although FindAGrave.com lists his year of birth as 1861), was forty-six or forty-seven at the time of his passing. His funeral service was held at the family home at 415 West Superior Street in Munising, where his family lived until at least the 1940 census, and was paid for with an insurance policy from the Modern Woodmen of America (an organization Genry was a member of). He was buried at the Maple Grove Cemetery in Munising, along with his wife, who passed in 1956; his sons, Patrick Shea (1855–1919), Frank H. (1905–1955) and Edward Stephen, a sergeant in the U.S. Army who served in World War II (1907–1995); and daughters, Agnes A. (1896–1929) and Johanna (1898–1980).

Joseph Prato served as acting keeper of the Grand Island North Lighthouse throughout 1908, with Robert C. Mackenzie serving as interim assistant. Neither are noted as serving at lighthouses before or after that year. Prato, who was born in New York in 1845, was also a corporal during the Civil War. After his death in 1925, he was buried at Maple Grove Cemetery in Munising, the same location as the Genry family.

Alf Evensen transferred from the Marquette Harbor Lighthouse, where he was serving as the assistant keeper, to stand as the principal keeper at Grand Island. He remained in that head position until 1925. Orrin P. Young, who had worked briefly at Grand Island in 1900 (and who was first assistant at Au Sable Light Station when Morrison's body was discovered), returned to Grand Island as first assistant keeper under Evensen until 1910. Three other assistants came and went over the next fifteen years, and according to

LighthouseFriends.com, "The characteristics of Grand Island [North] Light was changed on October 4, 1926, and the station became unwatched."

At the time of his death in 1951, Mather's own company had decimated about 80 percent of the island by logging the old-growth forest to the ground. Ten years later, the North Light was relocated from the top of its historic tower to a steel pole in the yard, and the lighthouse was vacated and eventually put up for sale. In 1972, Dr. Loren Graham purchased the light for his beloved wife, Pat, whose family first arrived on the island in the early 1880s. Thus began their heartfelt task of restoring the light as their family's summer home.

The federal government acquired much of the land on the island in 1990, and today, it is a recreational and historical site that welcomes visitors year round. According to the United States Department of Agriculture, Forest Service, the location of the Grand Island North Lighthouse (in the Hiawatha National Forest) on top of a 175-foot-tall cliff has been identified as the highest lighthouse above sea level in the United States. Grand Island Township is noted as the second-least-populated municipality in Michigan (after Pointe Aux Barques Township), and the entire island is designated as the Grand Island National Recreation Area.

Visitors can access the island via Grand Island Ferry Service (GrandIslandUP.com), which departs from Munising between May and October, as well as private watercraft (both motorized and sea kayaks). Camping, biking and hiking are allowed on the island, as are snowshoeing, cross-country skiing and snowmobiling in the winter months. The Grand Island Interpretive Bus offers narrated tours between Memorial Day and Labor Day, taking passengers to scenic overlooks, shoreline beaches, nature areas and historic sites, including the Cliff Cabin and the island's historic cemetery (but not the North Lighthouse, which is privately owned). In addition to the various rustic camp sites, a handful of cabins are also available through Grand Island Cabins (GrandIslandCabins.com).

10

PIE ISLAND LIGHTHOUSE

ONTARIO, CANADA

During its short history, only five men tended to the Pie Island Lighthouse in Lake Superior, located about six miles south of Thunder Bay and fifteen miles north of Isle Royale, Michigan. Of those men, two died during their service—both under mysterious circumstances.

Established in 1895, the original lighthouse was constructed on the west side of Pie Island (Île Pâté, or simply Le Pâté in French) and was later relocated by the dominion government to offer greater exposure from the north point of the island. According to Wikipedia, "Dominions were the semi-independent policies under the British Crown that constituted the British Empire, beginning with Canadian Confederation in 1867."

In the summer of 2020, the nonprofit group Canadian Lighthouses of Lake Superior (clls.ca) posted a historic photograph of the Pie Island Lighthouse on its Facebook page with a caption that read, in part: "Pie Island Light considered an alternate entrance to the port is situated at the mouth of Thunder Bay. For commercial traffic and for local boaters, Pie Island Light provided a marker to a passage for vessels from Duluth/Superior. When vessels were heading to the Thunder Bay Port, they'd first come to the Victoria Island Lighthouse and then pass Pie Island before reaching their destination."

Augustine W. Daby was commissioned to build the simple twenty-three-foot-tall, square, wooden tower for a mere $325. It was painted mostly white, with a red lantern room to house the fixed, white seventh-order Fresnel lens that shone out some ten miles into the fresh waters of Lake Superior. Sitting

The Pie Island Lighthouse, circa 1912. *Courtesy of the Library and Archives of Canada.*

on top of a rocky part of the shoreline, it was elevated twenty-nine feet above the lake level. Upon its completion, Daby served briefly as tender of the light for an annual salary of just $75.

Next was Thomas Hamilton, a single man in his mid-fifties who was appointed head keeper in 1899. During his tenure, the lighthouse was moved three-quarters of a mile north, up the coast, to the highest point of the island. A new dwelling was erected just fifty feet northeast of the light, and the entire project was supervised by W.H. Brunel of Ottawa for just under $500. It was in this simple home where Hamilton suffered a tragic death less than two years later.

The Tuesday, May 22, 1906 issue of the *Winnipeg Tribune* broke the news of Hamilton's passing: "Port Arthur, Ont.—Investigation by the coroner establishes that Thos. Hamilton, the keeper of Pie Island lighthouse, who was found dead on Saturday, had died of a hemorrhage. It is supposed that death came in the evening, as he had evidently died 10 days ago, and yet the light was burning up to Thursday evening. The island was visited on Saturday by fishermen, who discovered the ghastly sight of the poor old man lying on the floor of his house covered with blood."

A few days later, on May 25, 1906, the *Oswego Daily Times* (which was published in Oswego, New York, from 1887 until 1925) ran a story about the incident that was reprinted on LighthouseFriends.com: "Thomas Hamilton, lightkeeper for many years at Pie Island, was found dead at the lighthouse by Indians who went to take him provisions. He was sixty-nine years old, lived alone on the island and, when found, had apparently been dead for ten days."

There was no indication about what caused the deadly hemorrhage, as noted by Coroner Dr. Charles N. Laurie of Port Arthur; although one newspaper stated it was "natural causes."

Northern Wilds (NorthernWilds.com), a monthly magazine published along Lake Superior's north shore, noted a similar account written by Elle Andra-Warner on September 22, 2017: "In 1906, two First Nations men arrived on May 19 with provisions for 61-year-old Thomas Hamilton, who was single and had been the keeper since 1899. Sadly, they found Hamilton dead. On his death certificate, his death is listed due to a hemorrhage about May 12."

The First Nations and Indigenous Studies Program at the University of British Columbia notes, "'First Nation' is a term used to describe Aboriginal peoples of Canada who are ethnically neither Métis nor Inuit. This term came into common usage in the 1970s and '80s and generally replaced the term 'Indian,' although unlike 'Indian,' the term 'First Nation' does not have a legal definition."

Fort Williams was and is an Ojibwe reserve in Ontario, established as a result of the Robinson Treaty of 1850, the first of two treaties signed that year between Ojibwe chiefs and the Crown (Monarchy of Canada). Today, known as Thunder Bay, Fort Williams includes Pie Island, as well as Le Pâté Provincial Nature Reserve, which was created in 1853 and intended not only for the Ojibwe children of the time but also for their grandchildren's grandchildren who settled in the area.

A man with the surname Forbes was appointed as the next keeper, and while some records note that this didn't occur until 1908, newspaper accounts state he served six years—putting him into service immediately after Hamilton's passing. As for his first name, there are three that appear in various sources: James, Robert (which appears most commonly) and John (which is listed on the official death record). A married man, Forbes served at Pie Island Lighthouse until his tragic death on October 16, 1911.

The *Oakland Tribune*—published over 3,500 miles away in California—was one of the first to cover the situation, with a story under the headline "Suspected Indian Slayers Found Dead" the following day:

"WINNIPEG, Oct. 17—The finding of the body of Robert Forbes, an aged lighthouse keeper at Pie Island, 25 miles from Fort William, Ont., led the police to suspect Mose McCon, chief of a squaw band located north of Thunder Bay, and Fred Smith, another Indian, as being the murderers. A search for the Indians resulted in finding their bodies in a cabin on

STOLEN ALCOHOL KILLS MURDERERS

Canadian Indians Kill Old Keeper of Lighthouse, Drink Poison Used to Clean Lamp.

WINNIPEG, Man., Oct. 17.—The finding of the bzody of Robert Forbes, an aged lighthouse keeper at Pie Island, 25 miles for Fort William, Ont., led the police to suspect Mose McCon, chief of a Squaw band located north of Thunder Bay, and Fred Smith, another Indian as being the murderers. A search for the Indians resulted in finding their bodies in a cabin in Squaw Bay near Pie Island.

They had died from wood alcohol poisoning.

The alcohol it is believed was taken from the lighthouse, where it was kept to clean the lamp.

The *St. Louis Post Dispatch* ran one of several articles about the 1911 death of lighthouse keeper Robert Forbes. *Courtesy of the* St. Louis Post Dispatch.

Squaw Bay [on the mainland], near Pie Island. They had died from wood alcohol poisoning. The alcohol, it is believed, was taken from the lighthouse, where it was kept to clean the lamp."

Wood alcohol, also called methanol or methyl alcohol, is a type of industrial alcohol used today in pesticides, windshield wiper fluid, paint thinner, antifreeze and, back in the 1800s, a cleaning solvent that was commonly found in lighthouses. Early moonshine also contained methanol with high lead levels, as it was manufactured by distilling it through lead pipes, lead soldering or even car radiators during the Prohibition era.

The *Port Arthur New Chronicle* also ran an article on the front page of the October 17, 1911 issue that gave a bit more detail about Forbes's death under the headline "THREE DIE FROM WOOD ALCOHOL—KEEPER OF THE PIE ISLAND LIGHT AND TWO INDIANS ARE VICTIMS":

> *Xavier Francq, a stepson of Forbes, visited the light Sunday night and found the keeper in a state of collapse. He brought him to Fort William and took him to McKellar Hospital, where he died yesterday forenoon. In the meantime, the provincial police were informed of the circumstances by Francq, who gave it as his opinion that the two Indians had been engaged in a drinking bout. The officers then started a search for the Indians and, later in the day, found their bodies in a shack near the light.*
>
> *The bodies were moved to Fort William and a coroner's jury summoned by Dr. Birdsall. The jurymen viewed the bodies last evening and will take evidence tonight.*
>
> *Forbes was 75 years of age and has been for the past six years at the lighthouse, in fact, as long as the building has been erected and the light working. At this lonely point, 25 miles from this city, he has followed his occupation assiduously, until a short time ago, when it seems that he started indulging in alcohol. A stepson* [Francq] *who visited him a few days ago found him and two Indians drinking together, and it is said that he never recovered from the bout.*

It appears the deaths of all three men can be attributed to drinking this toxic alcohol, clearly not fit for human consumption. Their desperation for the euphoric effects of booze ultimately lead to their demise. As little as four milliliters of methanol has been known to cause blindness, and death can be caused by ingesting as little as thirty milliliters. The inquest into the deaths was organized by Dr. William Wallace Birdsall, a member of the Thunder Bay Medical Society.

Some ten days later, on October 27, 1911, an article appeared in the *Herald* that revealed an important detail about Forbes's body and an expressed statement of motive under the headline "MURDERERS FOUND DEAD. The Lighthouse Keeper Killed on Pie Island":

"A despatch [*sic*] from Sault Ste Marie, Ont., says: A party of hunters, who arrived here on Friday afternoon from the north shore, tell a strange story of what is believed to be the murder of Robert Forbes, a lighthouse keeper on Pie Island, twenty-five miles from Fort William. Forbes' body was found in his station on the island with the head battered in. The subsequent finding of the bodies of two Indians, who had died after drinking wood alcohol, is believed to explain the murder. It has been determined that the alcohol was taken from the lighthouse, and the police believe the Indians killed Forbes to get at the liquor, which they thought was good to drink. The Indians evidently drained a gallon cask of the poisonous liquid. Both were found lying side by side with the empty cask between them."

A copy of the death registration for John Forbes that was posted on Ancestry.com confirms that the seventy-five-year-old keeper died at McKellar General Hospital in Fort William (now Thunder Bay) as a result of "excessive drinking of whiskey and wood alcohol"—essentially, alcohol poisoning. There was no reference to head injuries, as noted in the previous article, nor was there any indication of murder at the hands of McCon and Smith. There is also no record of where he is buried.

The website LighthouseFriends.com notes that an X. Frank (likely Forbes's stepson Xavier Francq) was hired as a temporary keeper on October 16, 1911, until J. Vernon could assume control of the light the following year. Vernon served for ten years until the light was automated in 1926 and subsequently abandoned in the 1930s.

One online post said that the wooden tower from the Pie Island Light was auctioned off for a mere fifteen dollars, and the lumber, windows and doors were hauled southwest to Cloud Bay on the mainland to be repurposed in the construction of a private home. The website LighthouseFriends.com states:

The cornerstone for the John McKellar Memorial Hospital in Thunder Bay was laid on October 10, 1902. It was here that Robert Forbes died in 1911. *Courtesy of the Thunder Bay Public Library.*

"In 2010, the Department of Fisheries and Oceans announced its intention to demolish Pie Island Lighthouse. Besides disposing of the old wooden tower, the work was to include dismantling the concrete pier foundations and performing soil remediation at the site. Tenders for the demolition were to close on August 3, 2010, and the work was to be completed by mid-September, but fortunately, the destruction of the historic lighthouse was halted. Instead, the tower was spruced up and given a new coat of paint. Pie Island Lighthouse stands on Crown land that was transferred to Fort Williams First Nation [fwfn.com] in 2011 to settle a 160-year-old land claim. The lighthouse may be relocated in the future."

Today, over sixty acres on the western side of Pie Island is designated as the Le Pâté Provincial Nature Reserve. There are also a number of private summer cottages on the southern point of the island, which were not subjected to the land claim.

11

ST. IGNACE LIGHTHOUSE

TALBOT ISLAND, ONTARIO

It is said that when bad things happen, they often come in threes. Such was the case at the short-lived St. Ignace Lighthouse on Talbot Island in northern Lake Superior in the area of Upper Canada (as established in 1791 by the Kingdom of Great Britain).

Located on the southern shore of Nipigon Bay, the kidney bean–shaped St. Ignace Island—with an area of 106 square miles—is recognized as the eleventh-largest lake island in the world and the second largest in Lake Superior (following Isle Royale). It is also the fifth largest of all the islands in the Great Lakes region, behind Manitoulin, Isle Royale, St. Joseph Island and Drummond Island, respectively. To the east of the island is Nipigon Straits, which flows into Blind Channel and then Lake Superior, a dangerous passage for early mariners. Although uninhabited and unidentified, the large island was also depicted on a 1669 map attributed to French voyageurs Father Claude-Jean Allouez and Father Jacques Marquette.

Surrounding St. Ignace Island are countless other islands that make up the Lake Superior Archipelago, which measures 180 miles in length and includes other smaller island groupings. One of the lesser-known islands there, three miles south of the dominating St. Ignace Island, is Talbot Island. Long and narrow, it is said to be predominantly made up of forest and bedrock, with towering cliffs that disappear in the fog that often hovers over this area.

This region was well known before Jesuit priests and entrepreneurs arrived to establish the fur trade industry. According to a history post on

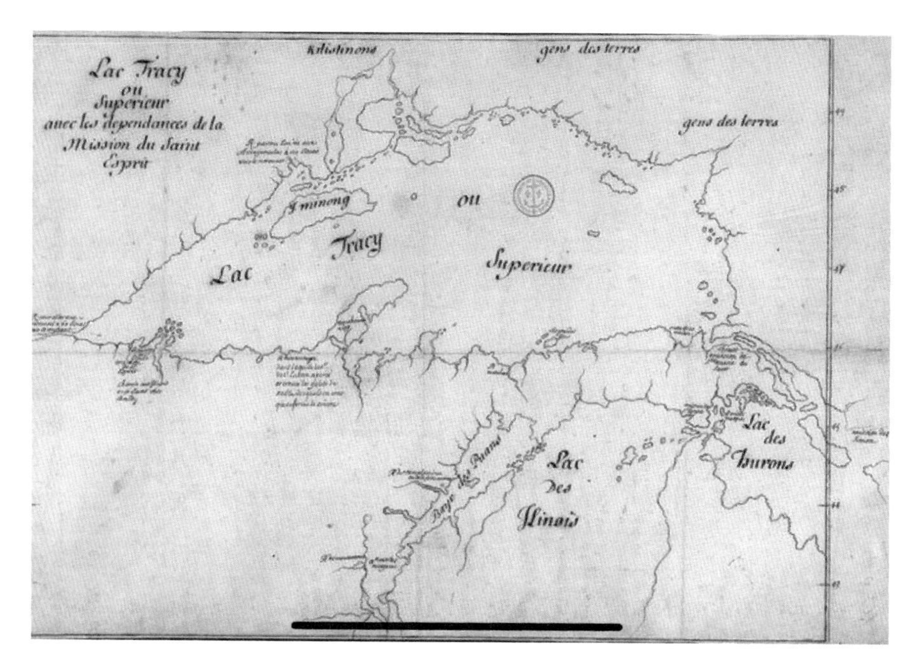

Although it was uninhabited and unidentified, the Talbot Island was depicted on a 1669 map attributed to French voyageurs Father Claude-Jean Allouez and Father Jacques Marquette. *Courtesy of Service Historique de la Défense, Département Marine, Cartes et Plans, R67 no. 76.*

Nipigon.com, Aboriginal people first arrived in here roughly nine thousand years ago. "It is possible that they survived off of big-game hunting and came into the area while following the caribou herds. There are rock paintings near the mouth of the Nipigon River which predate European contact by several thousand years."

The first permanent fur trading outpost was established in 1679 by French explorer Claude Greysolon Dulhut, followed by Pierre Gaultier de Varennes in the 1720s. The Hudson's Bay Company (HBC) built Fort Nipigon (Fort Ste. Anne) to protect its own fur operations, which had been established in 1859 as Red Rock House, along with a wharf to accommodate steamboats that were coming in to pick up goods for sale elsewhere. HBC's outpost was destroyed by fire in 1891, and its operations were moved elsewhere in the region. Ironically, Nipigon wasn't officially settled until 1909, but as an unincorporated area, it is regarded as one of the oldest communities on Ontario's Lake Superior north shore.

The year 1867 was big for this region of Canada. According to the Legislative Assembly of British Columbia (leg.bc.ca), "A federation of colonies in British North America—New Brunswick, Nova Scotia, Quebec, and Ontario—joined together to become the Dominion of Canada on July 1, 1867. Under the British North America Act, 1867, the queen remained head of state, represented nationally in Canada by the Governor General and in each province by a lieutenant governor. The British North America Act provided the constitutional framework for our current federal system by defining broad areas of federal and provincial jurisdiction. Such national matters as defence [*sic*], postal service, criminal law, and banks are under federal authority. Education, health, and natural resources are primarily among the provinces' responsibilities."

That summer, Canada's first Lake Superior lighthouse was constructed on Talbot Island to aid in navigation for vessels engaged in both fishing and fur trading. Situated on the east end of the island, the white, square, wooden tower sat on top of a stone foundation and was outfitted with three fixed, white lamps with a range of eight miles to guide vessels passing through the shoal-filled archipelago.

Apparently, the local Ojibwe who lived in this region warned government officials against this specific locale, claiming it was cursed and haunted by evil spirits. Whether that was the case or not, there is no question that this remote island lighthouse quickly earned the moniker "Lighthouse of Doom." During its brief seven years in operation, the St. Ignace Lighthouse had but three keepers. And tragically, all three died during the harsh winters of southern coastal Canada.

The first keeper appointed to the small lighthouse was William Perry, who lived there alone and recorded a successful first season. In November 1867, he packed his belongings and set out on a boat to the mainland near the HBC's post some twenty-five miles away to spend the winter, as was common for island keepers. But he never arrived. The "Gales of November" likely kicked up treacherous waves that tossed Perry and his boat around like a leaf in the wind. The following spring, his frozen body and capsized boat were found inland from the shore of Nipigon Bay, about fourteen miles from the HBC post, meaning he made a pretty good effort in getting to his destination before losing his life.

Thomas Lamphier (also spelled Lamphire, Lampheer or Lampshire) was married to a First Nations woman named Jane Sanders (or Saunders) from James Bay, Ontario. The couple had one child, a daughter named Elizabeth or "Betsy," of Métis-Cree descent in 1821 in the town of Moose Factory. The Canadian Museum of History (HistoryMuseum.ca) notes that "the Métis-Cree of Canada are the children of the Cree women and French, Scottish and English fur traders who were used to form alliances between

Native peoples and trading companies. We, the Métis, are a nation, sharing the traditions of all our mothers and fathers."

Lamphier was a longtime mariner on the waters of Lake Superior, having worked his way up the ranks of the Hudson's Bay Company between 1831 and 1862 aboard sloops *Union*, *Whitefish* and *Isabel*, where he served as skipper (1852–54) and sloopmaster (1856–62). During his service as captain of the *Whitefish*, a member of the crew—a Scotsman by the name of Alexander Clark—fell in love and subsequently married Lamphier's daughter, Betsy.

When he retired from the HBC, Lamphier took on a new career as a lighthouse keeper. In the summer of 1868, he and Jane moved to Talbot Island to take charge of the St. Ignace Lighthouse. Since Perry's passing, the Canadian government had expanded the residence and winterized both it and the tower at a cost of just under $650, according to LighthouseFriends.com. This meant the Lamphiers should have been able to ride out the winter on the island without risking their lives on dangerous voyages up to Nipigon Bay.

But Thomas Lamphier could not escape the hands of death that winter. He suddenly became ill, or perhaps fell and injured himself. Either way, he died, leaving Jane alone on the isolated island. What's more, she had to figure out how to deal with her husband's dead body. Even without the snow and ice that was accumulating on Talbot Island, the rocky ground made it nearly impossible to dig an appropriate grave for the dead keeper. And clearly it was much too hazardous for June to try to load her husband's body in their boat and make her way up to Nipigon Bay. Utilizing what she had at her disposal, Jane took the sail from their small boat and wrapped Thomas in it tightly before lodging his body in a crevice in the rocks behind the lighthouse. Then all she could do was return to their home and wait all alone, hoping the food and firewood would hold out until the spring thaw came.

Months later, some say as late as June, a group of passing Ojibwe noticed Jane's frantic signal for help and approached the shore of Talbot Island to find the once-beautiful woman looking gaunt, aged and at her wits' end. She told them of the heartbreaking ordeal that took her husband from her at the start of winter and led them to where she had hastily entombed his body. They agreed to take Thomas to nearby Bowman Island (just a mile away) for a proper burial. To this day, down a wooded path in a tiny clearing is a white cross with a plaque that reads, "In memory of Thomas Lampshire, Talbot Island lightkeeper, died 1869."

The third and final keeper of this unfortunate lighthouse was Andrew Hynes, who was hired for an annual salary of $400. He served longer than

The grave of lighthouse keeper Thomas Lamphier still stands on Bowman Island, a mile away from Talbot Island. *Courtesy of Lee Ann Lange, Bowman Island Lodge.*

any other keeper there (albeit he only served three years), coming in after Lamphier's death in 1869 and staying until his own passing at the end of the 1872 shipping season. Much like Perry five years prior, Hynes packed up his belongings at the end of the season and loaded them in the small boat assigned to the station to escape the island for the winter. His destination wasn't Nipigon Bay, it was Silver Islet, some fifty miles southwest of Talbot Island and the site of Canada's first major silver discovery in 1868, hence its name.

Once again, Lake Superior showed its fury and rage with an early-season storm that threw all its weight (and then some) on Hynes day after day. It is said he spent eighteen days out on the frigid waters, trying to reach the shore on Silver Islet at the tip of the Sibley Peninsula. When he did finally arrive, he was dehydrated, starving and exhausted, with a severe case of hypothermia. He didn't live long after that, succumbing to the beating he took spending two and a half weeks exposed to the elements.

Although Hynes was married, his wife thankfully didn't live with him on the island and thus escaped the horrific situation and ultimate end her husband met. In September 1873, Hynes's widow received a payment of $65.42 in wages (for April 1 to June 1), as well as $156.39 in arrearages owed to her husband, authorized by William Smith, the deputy of the minister of marine and fisheries, as noted in the "Sixth Annual Report of the Canada Department of Marine and Fisheries" for the year ending on June 30, 1873, printed by order of parliament (as well as the "Sessional Papers—Volume 3 of the First Session of the Third Parliament of the Dominion of Canada, 1874").

With three lighthouse keepers and three deaths, perhaps the Canadian government finally took heed of the warnings from the Ojibwe, as no other person was appointed to this light and it was subsequently decommissioned. In 1875, the Department of Marine and Fisheries authorized the building of two other regional lights: one on Battle Island and the other on Lamb Island, marking the eastern and western entrances to Nipigon Bay, respectively. The lights were delayed, but both were put into operation in 1877.

12

MICHIPICOTEN ISLAND LIGHTHOUSE

THUNDER BAY, ONTARIO

Tempting fate repeatedly is bound to catch up with you, especially when you're dealing with the temperamental winter waves of Lake Superior and an island that is rumored to have been haunted for centuries by an evil spirit. The first keeper of the remote Michipicoten Lighthouse pressed his luck not once, not twice, but three times before he was never seen again.

The word *Michipicoten* is an Anglicized version of the original Ojibwe word *Mishipikwadina*, meaning "big bluffs," in honor of the large hills towering near the river's mouth. It identifies a community, river and island, the third-largest island in Lake Superior at fourteen miles long and eight miles wide (just under 72,000 acres).

The Michipicoten First Nation's website (Michipicoten.com) notes that based on excavation of archaeological sites at the mouth of the Michipicoten River, "there has been an uninterrupted occupation of this region by the aboriginal people for 7,000 years or more." It is among these early people, known as "Michipicoute" or "Gens du Lac," that these first mysterious stories originated. The fall 1974 issue of *Canadian Frontier* featured a four-page article by Donald E. Pugh that shed light on the spirited island: "According to legend, a small group of Indians snowshoeing over winter ice to the island on a dark, bitterly cold mid-winter day, suddenly began running in terror towards the island as the ice mysteriously began to breakup. But the island, which had seemed so near, was said to drift away from the men, pushed by an evil wind, leaving the majority of the party to be drowned for their audacity in challenging the 'gods.' Thus commenced the strange legend of the haunted 'floating island.' Such fearsome legends were to grow."

Some of France's most notable voyageurs had ties to this area—from Jacques Cartier in the early 1500s to Samuel de Champlain and Étienne Brûlé—as they learned that the area was rich with copper. Champlain, an explorer and cartographer, even noted Michipicoten Island on a map of North America as early as 1632, and in the early eighteenth century, a French fur trading post was built at the river's mouth and was often referred to as "Fort Michipicoten." After the French were defeated in the War of 1812, they soon abandoned their fort, which later reopened under British rule, competing against fur trading outposts run by the Hudson's Bay Company and North West Company.

It was from this demographic that the next batch of tales was drawn, as Pugh continued:

> *Early fur traders heard tales of Naniboozoo—the Great Hare—which supposedly guarded the harbour into Michipicoten Island. This massive rocky promontory looming out of dark waters in the shape of a squatting Indian inspired fear and wonder. Gifts were regularly left near the rock by passing Indians to appease the strange creature's wrath or to gain his good favor. Fur trader Alexander Henry, forced to eat lichen moss after being trapped by a fearful gale for nine days on Superior's barren coastline, was bitterly blamed by the Indians. They believed the storm was purposely sent by Naniboozoo to punish the White men for failing to leave the usual gifts for Michipicoten's Great Hare.*

Even religious leaders of the era were well informed of the foreboding island and published stories in their annual reports known as the "Jesuit Relations," according to Pugh.

> *Early missionaries were astounded by Ojibway Indians' genuine refusal to approach the island or even to travel in its direction. Upon asking why, the missionaries were told the following legend: A group of four venturesome Ojibways, it was said, dared the hostile Manitou of the Island by visiting him. On reaching the Island, they rapidly picked up fine pieces of abundant native copper adoring the beach but were fearful of attacks by lynxes and hares as large as dogs, which were said to guard the island. Quickly, they entered their canoes and paddled away at full speed for the mainland with their copper treasure. But they had not avoided detection. Suddenly, a*

> *powerful voice, resounding like thunder from the sky, cried in great anger: "Who are these robbers carrying off from me my children's cradles and playthings?" Stricken with terror, one Indian died immediately, another died before reaching land, and a third died soon after. The remaining Ojibway related the horrible story while dying in agony. The superstitious Indians, the Jesuits recorded, so feared the island from that point on that in the memory of man, no one has been known to set foot there or even be willing to sail in that direction. Indeed, as late as the 1850s, enterprising miners found themselves forced to wade ashore, since all the Ojibways, deathly afraid of Michipicoten's evil spirits, refused to touch that possessed ground.*

Over the years, brave souls continued to find their way to Michipicoten Island, lured by the prospects of all that copper. Yet, one calamity after another befell them, and they often left empty-handed, poorer than when they arrived and with horrific stories about the experience.

The curse of Michipicoten Island carries over into the waters surrounding it as well, as the area is reputed to be inhabited by the "memogovissioois," malevolent demons that live underwater like fish. Whether it was something unseen but nefarious or simply the shallow bays, rocky reefs, shoals and Lake Superior's inconsistent temperament, several vessels and a lighthouse keeper have fallen victim to the waters around the island.

With the fur trading, mining and subsequent boating traffic, it is interesting that Michipicoten Island itself didn't receive a lighthouse until 1911 (maybe they were afraid to build one there). Tiny Agate Island, tucked inside Quebec Harbour, received its lighthouse in the 1870s, but it clearly didn't prevent ships from sinking.

The *Free Lance* out of Fredericksburg, Virginia, on November 17, 1896, noted one such incident near the mainland and Michipicoten River under the headline "Sailors in Distress":

> *The Canadian steamer* Acadia, *which has been missing for several days, is ashore on the rocks near Michipicoten River and will be a total loss. The master of the steamer, Captain Clifford, with four of the crew, reached the port in a sailboat belonging to the lighthouse department. Since a week ago Thursday, they have been fighting for life against cold and hunger in the bleak desolate wilds on the Canadian shore of Lake Superior.*
>
> *The* Acadia *measured 806 tons and was owned in Hamilton, Ont. Her cargo was 20,000 bushels of wheat, the boat clearing from Fort William on Wednesday last week.*

> *"We are headed for shelter at Michipicoten River when a heavy snowstorm set in, and at 10 o'clock Thursday night, we struck the rocks," said Captain Clifford. "The sea increased, and soon after midnight, we were compelled to abandon the steamer. Our crew of 17 men took a supply of provisions and bedding ashore in the boats. We constructed a rude shelter on the beach near the steamer and remained there two days. The weather was very cold, and all hands suffered. There was no habitation within many miles, and the weather moderated after two days, and, leaving two men to watch the steamer, the remaining 15 got into the two yawl-boats and started for the nearest port.*
>
> *"The boats were laden with men and provisions. We arrived at Gargentua Saturday night. Leaving enough provisions, four of us embarked in the lighthouse tender, a sailboat, Sunday morning to make a desperate attempt to reach Sault Ste. Marie. But we struck heavy weather near Mamainoe. We were forced to land again. The desolate character of the country continued, and our provisions ran low. Fortunately, a settlement was discovered, and we obtained food.*
>
> *"The weather moderated yesterday, and we reached port all right. I am afraid the men left at Gargentua will suffer from hunger if we are not able to reach them in a short time. There are 11 men there, and their provisions will last them only two days longer."*
>
> *Captain Chamberlain and the members of his crew will leave at once, if the weather permits, for the scene of the wreck. On the way, he will pick up the men at Gargentua. An effort will be made to rescue the steamer, if anything can be done for her.*

The remains of six shipwrecks can be found around the Michipicoten Island. Four rest in the waters of Quebec Harbour in the southcentral part of the island: *J.S. Seaverns*, sunk May 10, 1884 (found in 2016); *Hiram R. Dixon*, which burned in 1903; *Billy Blake*, which caught fire in the 1940s; and *Big Jim*. Two lie west of Michipicoten Island: *Strathmore*, November 8, 1906; and *Chicago*, October 23, 1909.

After so many shipwrecks in such a short period, the Lake Carriers' Association (which was founded in 1880 to represent U.S.-flagged vessel operations on the Great Lakes), in 1908, petitioned to have lights and fog signals installed at both the east and west ends of Michipicoten Island. It would take three years for the Department of Marine to authorize a light on the island's east end. In 1911, an eighty-three-foot-tall, hexagonal concrete tower was erected (operating a third-order Fresnel lens), along with a keeper's

The *J.S. Seaverns* before it sank in 1884 near Michipicoten Island in Lake Superior. *Courtesy of the C. Patrick Labadie Collection at Thunder Bay National Marine Sanctuary.*

house, oil building and boathouse, located just under forty miles from the mainland of Michipicoten and Wawa within the Algoma provisional judicial district of northeastern Ontario.

The first keeper of the Michipicoten East End Lighthouse was William Wright Sherlock (also published Shirlock or Hurlock), who was born on October 29, 1871, on Prince Edward Island, Canada, to Henry Adolphus and Abigail (McArthur) Sherlock. He and his wife, Mary Christina "Minnie" Brown (or LeBraun), were married on March 28, 1894, in Port Arthur, and they had thirteen children between 1895 and 1913, including four sons and nine daughters.

As was customary for island keepers, Sherlock was given the option of staying within the confines of his lighthouse or heading to a mainland house to ride out the snowy months until the shipping season resumed in the spring. Being of frugal mind, he chose to remain island-bound instead of making his way to Sault Ste. Marie (more than 225 miles south), where the cost to rent the house created a financial burden for Sherlock and his large family.

Apparently, his decision to stay on Michipicoten Island was a big deal, as he was one of just two island keepers gearing up to winter in that remote region of Lake Superior that winter, and the *Gazette* out of Montreal published an article about the men on December 17, 1913:

> *Preferring to spend the coming winter in lonely lighthouses very much isolated in the bleak expanse of Lake Superior, rather than pay high rent and bring charges on, two lighthouse keepers in the employ of the Marine Department furnish one of the most unique examples of the pressure of the high cost of living which has yet come to light in Canada.*

Marine Department records today disclosed that for the first time on record, lighthouse keepers on two of the most forbidding spots in the big lake have made preparations to spend the winter there. They have given as their reason their disinclination to cope with the high cost of living on the mainland at Sault Ste. Marie this year. They propose to escape its demands by spending some five months where rent, at least, is a negligible factor, since no landlord can possibly come to collect it, and where the only bills to be presented will be those of occasional sea gulls.

The two lighthouses where cobwebs won't accumulate this winter are at East End, a station on Michipicoten Island and Corbell Point. William Sherlock, navigation's human aid at East End, is the man who is going to make the most lake history, since the station is a singularly forbidding spot some ten miles from the mainland, which, in Lake Superior winter, practically means 10 miles from nowhere.

Mr. W.H. Noble of the Marine Department, in his report as to the annual taking off of the lighthouse keepers, states that he reached East End in the steamer Premier *after much difficulty and took off the keeper's father-in-law and mother-in-law, Mr. and Mrs. Brown, who were not apparently prepared to spend five months in the "frost king's" keeping. Sherlock, the keeper, however, was left with his family well supplied with provisions and other necessaries.*

The Marine Department has refused to allow any of its keepers to spend the winter alone for obvious reasons, and does with reluctance in any case, as in an exposed station like East End, the occupants will be cut off from medical aid, and, in fact, all other human aid. Cases have occurred in saltwater stations where death took place during the winter and burial was impossible 'till spring.

Unless the weather changes, Sherlock is already committed to his voluntary imprisonment on Michipicoten Island, since lake navigation has closed and is probably now making preparations for a most unique Christmas.

The Sherlocks fared well throughout the winter months that season, although there is no indication of how things went or if they made this a winter tradition or a one-time occurrence. One major change to operations came down from the Marine Department in 1915, as it would no longer provide transportation to and from the light stations at the start and end of the season, meaning keepers (and their families) would have to travel under their own power in a government-issued eighteen-foot-long boat. Imagine how many trips that would take with a family the size of Sherlock's.

Now, by most accounts, things on the island seemed to be quiet for the next couple years—at least nothing newsworthy occurred until the winter of 1916, when Sherlock and his nineteen-year-old son, James, narrowly escaped death during an eight-day crossing of the treacherous waters of Lake Superior in that small lighthouse boat in the middle of December. Sherlock recounted the harrowing story with a writer for the *Sault Star* once they finally arrived safely on land. The story appeared under the headline "Lighthouse Men are Almost Frozen Coming to Sault" on December 28, 1916:

> *We left the lighthouse on the 14th of the month, because our docks had been swept away by the ice and the seas, and we saw that if we waited any longer, we wouldn't be able to get out. We started at two in the afternoon in an eighteen-foot boat, and after we had gone about 14 miles, we ran into a northeaster. Our pump froze, and we had to take to the oars. It was 12 degrees below zero at Gargantua that night. Our boat began to take in water, and we gradually had to throw everything we had away to keep afloat. First, we threw away 25 gallons of oil, then an emergency sail we were carrying and, finally, our provisions. Our bodies were caked in ice, and we could hardly bend either our legs or arms. One of the oars slipped away from my son in the afternoon, and he reached for it but slipped over the side of the boat; but fortunately, I grabbed him and got him out of the water.*
>
> *Then I thought I could hear something, and after listening for a while, I could hear the surf. In a short time, we struck Leach Island, where we made a fire. We were there for three days without anything to eat except a few biscuits that we saved out of the ice in the boat.*
>
> *The boat was in pretty bad condition, but I fixed it up as well as I could, and we left Leach Island at 4:30 in the afternoon of the 18th. We struck out for the North Shore, which was three miles distant, my son at the oars and I bailing all the way. There was not much of a sea, but it was bitterly cold and the wind was quite high. We finally struck the North Shore after five hours between Gargantua and Telegram Rock. There was a hill a short distance away, and my son crawled to it, from which point he could see the islands laying off Gargantua. All the time, we were carrying with us a puppy, which we had brought up in the spring. We killed him when we struck the North Shore, and this kept us alive until we struck Gargantua. We could only travel very slowly, and we had to crawl most of the way. Between us and Gargantua, there were a number of bluffs, and we had to go around most of these. We finally arrived on the 22nd. We left with Charley Miron, the lighthouse keeper, there and arrived in the city Tuesday night.*

The next season, William and James weren't so lucky when they set sail in mid-December. The *Manitoba Free Press* ran a story nearly three weeks later, on January 4, 1918, under the headline "Keeper of Lighthouse And Son, Both Missing":

"Some anxiety is felt by officials of the Marine Department here for the safety of William M. [*sic*] Sherlock, a lighthouse keeper of Michipicoten Island, Lake Superior, and his son, James, who have been missing since Dec. 15. On Dec. 27, George Johnson, who keeps the lighthouse station at Caribou Island [about twenty-seven miles south of Michipicoten Island] reported by telegraph that he could find no trace of the Sherlocks and that their station appeared to be deserted. It is feared that Sherlock and his son left the lighthouse, possibly to journey to the other end of the island, where there is a small settlement, and got lost or frozen to death. Communication between the island and the mainland is cut off at this season, and the Marine Department may not be able to secure definite information in regard to the men until spring. It is possible that they reached the station in safety. Sherlock's family live in Sault Ste. Marie."

The bodies of William and James were never recovered, and Minnie took over as the keeper of the East End Light until 1925 and died on October 27, 1931 (she was buried in Agawa Rocks, Ontario). William's older brother Henry "Melvin" Sherlock later became a keeper at the Michipicoten East End Lighthouse, serving from 1974 to 1981.

Minnie Sherlock, the wife of deceased Michipicoten East End Lighthouse keeper William Wright Sherlock, stepped into the position following his 1918 death until her retirement in 1925. *Courtesy of Ginny Miller.*

It was during Melvin's tenure that one of Great Lakes' most noted shipwrecks occurred just over seventy-five miles southeast of Michipicoten Island. The *Edmund Fitzgerald* left the Burlington Northern Railroad Dock in Superior, Wisconsin, at 8:30 a.m. on November 9, 1975, fully loaded with 26,116 tons of taconite (ore) pellets and headed to a steel mill on Zug Island, near Detroit. Captain Ernest M. McSorley was at the helm, leading his crew of twenty-eight men through Lake Superior, the largest and northernmost of the Great Lakes (and the world's largest lake by surface area).

That afternoon, the National Weather Service issued gale warnings for the area, and by early the next morning, a massive November storm was churning up the deep waters of Lake Superior with winds up to fifty-two knots and waves ten feet high. At 1:40 p.m., McSorley notified Captain Jesse Cooper aboard the *Arthur M. Anderson* that he had just cleared Michipicoten Island and that his ship was "rolling some" in the waves.

At this point, the *Anderson* was trailing the *Fitz* by some sixteen or seventeen miles. The two ships communicated off and on that afternoon, with the *Anderson* offering radar support for the distressed *Fitzgerald* as it neared Whitefish Point. Unfortunately, with the storm, the radio beacon and light at Whitefish was not operating, and McSorley was cruising blindly into the darkness.

Around 7:10 p.m., the *Anderson* messaged the *Fitzgerald* in what would become their last conversation.

> Anderson: Fitzgerald, *we are about 10 miles behind you and gaining about 1½ miles per hour.* Fitzgerald, *there is a target 19 miles ahead of us. So, the target would be 9 miles on ahead of you.*
> Fitzgerald: *Well, am I going to clear?*
> Anderson: *Yes. He is going to pass to the west of you.*
> Fitzgerald: *Well, fine.*
> Anderson: *By the way,* Fitzgerald, *how are you making out with your problem?*
> Fitzgerald: *We are holding our own.*

Sometime between 7:20 and 7:30 p.m., the *Fitzgerald* disappeared from the *Anderson*'s radar and slipped below the lake's surface, ultimately coming to rest on the bed of Lake Superior and taking all of its twenty-nine men to a watery grave.

The Michipicoten East End Lighthouse was automated in 1983 and later designated as a heritage structure by the Department of Fisheries and Oceans. The last active keeper there was John Louis Brandon, who concluded his service in 1988. The lighthouse remains active, flashing white every ten seconds with a signal visible for fourteen miles. The tower isn't open to the public; however, the grounds are accessible, with camping nearby at Cozens Cove.

In 1918, the Agate Island Lighthouse was moved to the mainland in Quebec Harbour as a Front Range Light, and a forty-two-foot-tall light was built six hundred feet inland as the Rear Range Light. Around this time, the Purvis Point Lighthouse was replaced by a new ninety-two-foot-tall light on Davieaux Island (formerly known as Long Island).

Today, the uninhabited Michipicoten Island is a recreational paradise, with opportunities for hiking, paddling, diving, fishing, camping and snowshoeing throughout the Michipicoten Island Provincial Park. There are about thirty interior lakes on the island, which are surrounded by lava flows and rocks, as well as sandy beaches, like Driftwood Beach. In the early 1980s, woodland caribou were introduced to the island, and the beaver population there is among the highest in the region.

In addition to the lighthouse and shipwrecks, historic sites on the island include the Quebec Harbour Fishing Camp, established in 1839 by the Hudson's Bay Company. All that remains is a small group of dilapidated buildings—a far cry from the area's "peak" population of seventy in the early to mid-twentieth century.

The abandoned Quebec Mines, which harvested copper from 1853 until around 1880, is another popular place to explore, as rusted equipment is scattered around the area. A note of caution: there are several open mine shafts hidden beneath fallen logs, shrubs and brush, so visitors are advised to keep a close eye on where they walk.

A handful of tour companies operate on the mainland, making Michipicoten Island accessible by boat or plane.

PART VI.

COMPILATION

13

OTHER LIVES LOST AT GREAT LAKES LIGHTHOUSES

During their service, many keepers lost their lives—some in more graphic ways than others, but they were all tragic, nonetheless. Some found their way to watery graves when the vessels they were traveling aboard capsized within the deep waters of the Great Lakes. Others, in their attempts to ride out the frigid winters in desolate locales, became victims of Mother Nature's cold hands. Some simply passed away at their beloved lights due to natural causes, but given the timing or location, even those instances seemed more unfortunate.

Lake Ontario

One of the most dreadful disasters in Great Lakes Coast Guard history took place on December 4, 1942, in the waters around New York's **Oswego Harbor West Pierhead Lighthouse**. Six guardsmen drowned when strong winds capsized their boat about a mile offshore as they attempted to assist a crew marooned at the lighthouse.

Those who were killed included lieutenant and commanding officer of the Oswego Coast Guard Station, Alston J. Wilson (fifty-four); Karl A. Jackson, boatswain's mate first class (forty-two); Leslie J. Holdsworth, seaman first class (twenty-one); Ralph J. Sprau, machinist's mate second class (twenty-seven); O. Irving Ginsburg, seaman second class (twenty-one); and Eugene C. Sisson, boatswain's mate second class (twenty-nine).

Five additional guardsmen were seriously injured in the accident, according to an article that appeared the following day in the *North Adams Transcript*, which read, "All were tossed against a 10-foot ice-covered breakwater yesterday when the motor of a 38-foot patrol launch stalled half a mile from shore. The boat, returning from landing two relief men on a lighthouse, was crushed."

Two of the men, Fred Ruff and John Mixon, were among the survivors. After being thrown deep into the frigid lake waters, they dragged themselves onto the breakwall and crawled on their bellies over the slippery blocks of ice to the shore, where they were eventually rescued and treated for exposure.

More information about this incident can be found in the booklet *Voices in the Storm—The Captivating True Story of the Courage of Brave Men*, by Michael J. Colasurdo.

LAKE ERIE

Benajah Wolcott had built up quite a resume by the time he was appointed the first keeper of the **Marblehead Lighthouse** in Ohio. Built in 1820, it is the oldest continuously operating lighthouse on Great Lakes.

Benajah Wolcott, the first keeper of Ohio's Marblehead Island Lighthouse in Lake Erie, died of cholera and was buried in a family plot not far from his family farm. *Courtesy of Debra Mock Brown.*

The Connecticut-born Wolcott was a Revolutionary War veteran (enlisting in the army at the age of fourteen and serving until he was twenty-two years old), a fiddle player and a surveyor of land along Lake Erie. In 1809, he bought 114 acres on what is now called Marblehead Peninsula, becoming one of the earliest settlers in the area. He brought with him his wife, Elizabeth, their three children and two hired men. Their time there was short-lived, as the War of 1812 loomed, and the family feared invasion by the British and their Native allies. So, the Wolcotts moved south to Newburgh, Ohio, on the Cuyahoga River. Sadly, Elizabeth died during this time, but in 1815, Benajah and the children moved back to their farm.

On March 1, 1822, Wolcott married Rachel Miller, and three months later, he was appointed keeper of the newly completed lighthouse on Marblehead. A farmer by trade, Wolcott maintained a home at the lighthouse, as well as a farm three miles away for his family. Both historic sites are still standing and open to the public.

Wolcott racked up ten years of service at the Marblehead Lighthouse before he contracted cholera and died on August 11, 1832, in his late sixties. According to FindAGrave.com:

> *People would dump dead bodies into Lake Erie for quick disposal. They, in turn, would wash up on the shores around the lighthouse. Benajah was infected by his contact with these victims during his compassion to provide proper burials. He was interred in the small family cemetery a short distance from the old stone house, which he constructed for his bride Rachel in 1822. His son William died about the same time and it is assumed by the same infection which claimed his father.*

LAKE MICHIGAN

The Sunday, October 20, 1901 issue of the *St. Joseph Gazette* ran a brief story about an autumn storm that took the lives of two keepers from the **Skillagalee Island Lighthouse**. Located nearly eight miles southwest of Waugoshance Shoal, on the east side of the approach to the Gray's Reef Passage, the light was built in 1888 and was also known as Ile Aux Galets Light, or "isle of pebbles."

Keeper Garret Bourissau and his assistant, Walter Grubbins, perished near Cross Village, where they had traveled to pick up supplies on October 18. They attempted to return to the island by sailboat when they encountered heavy seas, and the men were tossed around. "The boat came ashore at Cross

Andrew "Garret" Bourissau, keeper of the Skillagalee Island Lighthouse in northern Lake Michigan, died in October 1901, when his sailboat was caught in a storm between Cross Village and Skillagalee Island. His body was never found. *Courtesy of the U.S. Lighthouse Society.*

Village today with the body of Grubbins lashed to the rigging, but no trace of Bourissau has been found. Isadore Lacroix, the third member of the crew, was left at the lighthouse, and it has not been possible to notify him of the fate of his companions."

One of the most commonly shared stories from this area was the Friday, December 14, 1900 accident involving the keepers and family members from the **Squaw Island Lighthouse** in the northern Beaver Island Archipelago. The light sits on a seventy-five-acre island on the western edge of Gray's Reef Passage, the main route between the Straits of Mackinac and Lake Michigan's western and southern harbors.

On the day in question, head keeper William Harrison Shields loaded up his wife, Mary A. (LaCroix), and niece (Lucy Davis); along with his first assistant, Owen C. McCauley; his second assistant, Lucien Morden; his faithful dog; and many of their belongings into a twenty-five-foot-long, two-masted sailboat to head to Beaver Island some nine miles away for the winter. The trip should have taken about two hours under normal conditions, but there was nothing normal about that day.

A fifteen-plus-page first-person account written by McCauley just prior to his retirement from the U.S. Lighthouse Service in 1936 provided the horrific details. It was published under the title "Death in Icy Waters" and printed in vol. 5 of the *Journal of Beaver Island History*.

A squall came up, hitting the sails and laying the boat over on its side, the sails flat on the water. A panic set in, with the men trying to keep themselves out of the freezing water while also trying to assist the women.

"Shields clung to his wife, and Morden held fast to Mrs. Davis. I grasped Morden around the waist, and by doing so, it braced him so that he pulled Mrs. Davis up on the center board box, and then I assisted him in getting her braced up on the boat so that she could be tied," McCauley wrote. "Morden took hold of the fore sheet and tied it around the waist of Mrs. Davis. As I saw that this would not hold her up, I went down in the water and cut a part of one of the sails halyards long enough to dip it under the center board and tied it behind her back; this braced her so that she could not fall away. Her feet stood on the center board box, and her arms laid over the boats side. Shields, in the meantime, lashed his wife with the stern sheet."

As the hours passed and darkness set in, conditions continued to deteriorate. Lucy was the first to pass, and soon, Mrs. Shields became delirious and "begged of her husband to cut her loose, as she wanted to be relieved from unendurable suffering, but he refused her entreaties." McCauley continued, "When she saw that her request was ignored, she asked him to grant her a last request to lower her body or cut the ties that held her fast after she would die, as she did not want her lifeless body to be exposed to the fury of the elements. We assured her that her last request would be granted." The woman, described as having a large stature with a robust constitution, succumbed shortly thereafter to the elements, leaving just the three men.

Morden was the next to pass, his frozen and numb body slipping below the water after he untied himself from the boat in an apparent attempt to end his life and avoid further pain and suffering. Shields and McCauley rode out the night, the bodies of the women still tied to the boat (despite a promise made to Mrs. Shields on her deathbed to cut her loose).

Eventually the steamer *Manhattan* appeared in the distance, and it was apparent that the long ordeal was nearly over. Both men and the bodies

The steamer *Manhattan* came upon the sailboat where Squaw Island Lighthouse keeper William Shields and assistant keeper Owen McCauley were clinging to life in December 1900. *Courtesy of the Historical Collections of the Great Lakes at Bowling Green State University.*

of the women were loaded aboard the vessel and taken to the Holy Family Hospital in Manitowoc, Wisconsin.

The forty-six-year-old Shields suffered from frostbitten hands and feet and had to have one of his legs amputated at the knee, while one side of his body was partially paralyzed. He remained hospitalized for more than six months, but he eventually returned to lighter duty at the mainland Charlevoix Light Station. He served until April 1924 and passed away the following September, around the age of seventy or seventy-one. Both Shields and his wife were buried in the Holy Childhood of Jesus Cemetery in Harbor Springs, Michigan.

McCauley's wife, Mary, who was pregnant with their daughter, Clementine, at the time of the accident, anxiously waited weeks before she got word that her thirty-one-year-old husband had survived and would be leaving the hospital fully recovered. McCauley was promoted to the head keeper position at Squaw Island the following spring, and he remained there until the light closed in 1928. He was then transferred to the St. Joseph Lighthouse in southern Lake Michigan, serving until his retirement in 1936, after nearly forty years in the business. He died on September 14, 1958, at the U.S. Public Health Service Hospital at the age of eighty-nine and was buried in the Resurrection Cemetery in St. Joseph, Michigan.

A coroner's jury conducted an inquisition surrounding the accident and subsequent deaths but ultimately ruled that nature caused the accident and that no keepers would be blamed for the tragedy.

On Christmas Eve in 1967, John Marken and his wife, Beatrice "Bea" (Doyle), were heading back to their home at the **Grand Traverse Lighthouse** in Northport, at the tip of the Leelanau Peninsula, when their car veered off the road and struck a tree. They were killed instantly and were among twenty-one people who lost their lives on Michigan roads that holiday weekend.

Marken began his service as a quartermaster aboard the tender *Marigold* in 1939 and later served as first assistant keeper at the Mackinac Point Lighthouse (1951–57) before transferring to Grand Traverse as the head keeper in 1958.

The couple had gone into town for a holiday gathering and were on their way home that Sunday evening when the accident occurred on the dead-end road about a quarter of a mile from the lighthouse. According to an article in the *Traverse City Record Eagle* (December 26, 1967), "Leelanau county sheriff's department said the bodies were found at 8:45 a.m. Monday by Sterling Nickerson, another lighthouse employee. The department said it was determined the couple died instantly in the crash and that the accident probably occurred about 8:20 p.m. Sunday."

John was sixty-one years old at the time of his death in 1967; Bea was fifty-nine. Ray Martinson Funeral Home in Suttons Bay handled the local funeral arrangements, and the couple was buried at the Riverside Cemetery in Sault Ste. Marie, Michigan.

The Grand Traverse Lighthouse is open to the public during the summer months. It is located inside the Leelanau State Park, and a Michigan State Passport is required for entry.

One of the most noted keeper families on South Manitou Island was the Sheridans—Aaron and his wife, Julia. Following his service in the Civil War, the disabled veteran (who lost the use of his left arm after all the bones were shattered during the Battle of Ringgold Gap) was appointed keeper of the very important **South Manitou Island Lighthouse** in the summer of 1866.

For twelve years, Aaron and Julia and their six sons lived and worked at the lighthouse, keeping the third-order Fresnel lens at the top of the one-hundred-foot-tall tower illuminated. Things seemed perfect for the Sheridans until March 15, 1878, when Aaron, Julia and their nine-month-old son, Robert, drowned after their boat capsized on a return trip to the island. Christen Ancharson, a local fisherman who had sailed them to the mainland and back, was the only survivor.

The bodies of the three Sheridans were never recovered, but in 2006, descendants of the family placed memorial markers in the South Manitou Island Cemetery in honor of Aaron, Julia and Baby Robert. They can be found in the far-left corner of the cemetery, not far from the ferry dock.

For more on this story, check out chapter 3 of *Michigan's Haunted Lighthouses*. The second-oldest Sheridan son, George, went on to become a lighthouse keeper himself. His tragic story can be found in chapter 8 of this book.

Gustavus Amiel Umberham, keeper of the Algoma Pierhead Lighthouse in Wisconsin, was lost at sea in February 1913. *Courtesy of the U.S. Lighthouse Society via the Great Lakes Lighthouse Keepers Association.*

Gustavus Amiel Umberham (also printed Uubehaun) began his lighthouse service career in 1884, when he was hired as a first assistant at the Poverty Island Lighthouse. He spent twenty-nine years at various lights, including the St. James Habor Lighthouse on Beaver Island (1886–90); Cedar River Lighthouse, between Menominee and Escanaba (1890–1901); and **Algoma Pierhead Lighthouse** (previously known as the Ahnapee Light) at the eastern base of Door County, Wisconsin (1901–13).

A detailed story on LighthouseDigest.com, written by publisher Timothy Harrison, includes a wealth of details about Umberham's personal life, including four wives, more than eighteen children (and stepchildren) and his death at the age of fifty-two.

> *On that tragic night in February* [3,] *1913, as the* Reliance *cut its way through the bitter cold winter water of Lake Michigan, the weather suddenly worsened. As heaving waves pitched the boat, the cabin windows soon became covered in ice. The men opened the windows but still found it almost impossible to see where they were going as the cold wind blew fiercely and icy spray would splash up through the openings. They tried to use the compass, but the lantern they used to illuminate it went out. They were about six miles south of Algoma Harbor and were now navigating mostly by their wits alone with some guidance from the few lights along the distant shoreline.*
>
> *After standing his watch, Gus came inside the cabin to warm up before he went to relieve William Adamson at the helm. Suddenly, a high wave struck the boat, and he must have lost his balance, pitching him into the cabin door with such force that the door came off its hinges and toppled him head-long into Lake Michigan.*
>
> *Realizing what had happened, the men immediately turned the boat around to look for Gus. Twice, they heard him cry for help, but in the darkness of the night, they could not see or find him. They turned the engine off in hopes that they could better hear his cries, but to no avail. For the next hour, they circled around, turning the engine on and off to search for him, but they soon realized that all hope was lost.*

Umberham's body was never recovered, but over the years, his children made attempts to find his remains. Harrison noted that the family would travel to various shoreline locations when there was a report of an unidentified body found, hoping it would be the lost keeper.

His son Amiel Umberham even initiated his own investigation sparked by a 1920 article regarding a body found in 1915 that may or may not have been his father, based on its apparent age and decomposition. However, the nameless body was buried in a pauper's field, later to be claimed, exhumed and reinterred by the local Independent Order of Odd Fellows as one of their missing members named Joseph Peppan. In another twist, years later, Peppan was found to be living in California, and the identity of the buried body, as well as the location of the grave, remains unknown. Perhaps if that information is ever discovered, the body could be exhumed once again for DNA testing against living descendants of Gus Umberham.

In late February 1855, Michael Green, who had been a keeper for nine years at the **Bailey's Harbor Lighthouse** in Door County, Wisconsin, died after his boat capsized while en route to Green Bay to pick up his paycheck and mail letters. According to news accounts, a party of Norwegians (later identified as Reverend Mr. Everson and his companions) who were on their way to Milwaukee came upon an unidentified man in distress and took him to an uninhabited shanty along the shore for care.

A letter to the editor of the *Door County Advocate* appeared as part of a larger article in the March 17, 1855 issue of the *Manitowoc Herald*. It provided further details about the recovery and identification of the body: "All was done for him that could be by the two who remained with him, while the others came to our station to procure assistance, which was sent as soon as possible—but too late; the poor fellow died about sundown last evening. The body was brought to this place this evening and will be interred tomorrow. A small leather satchel containing a package of letters and two shirts was found by him. The letters have been forwarded to your post office to-day. From papers found on his person, we were induced to believe that he was keeper of the lighthouse at Bailey's Harbor. But persons here who have examined him think it is Michael Green of your place."

Lake Superior

On February 10, 1910, two assistant keepers at the **Split Rock Lighthouse** in Two Harbors, Minnesota, died when their rowboat capsized while they were en route to retrieve the mail. Apparently, the boat had been found, but there was no trace of the men's bodies. Edward F. Sexton (first assistant) and Roy C. Gill (second assistant) worked for head keeper Orrin Young as the first staff of this newly constructed light perched on a cliff 130 feet above the waters below. One newspaper account noted that W.H. Gill, Roy's brother (and assistant keeper of the Saginaw River Range Light), had "offered a reward of $5 for the recovery of the body," as "dragging operations have failed to bring it to the surface."

Pliny F. Rumrill was serving as the principal keeper (and his wife, Matilda, as assistant keeper) at the **Michigan Island Lighthouse** in Wisconsin's remote Apostle Islands in September 1878, when their teenage son William H. or "Willie" died off the coast of the island. Some online sources note that the incident actually occurred near Outer Island, but the Rumrills never served there. Either way, on the day in question, Willie apparently entered the water to retrieve a boat that had gone adrift when he was consumed by cramps and drowned before anyone could rescue him. He was buried in Greenwood Cemetery in Bayfield, Wisconsin.

Reuben Hart hadn't been a lighthouse keeper for very long. He began his career in 1880 on Huron Island, where he served as a second and then first assistant before being promoted to principal keeper at **Manitou Island Lighthouse** on October 26, 1881. He served just eight months until his death on May 19, 1882. The website TerryPepper.com provides dated logbooks with two entries regarding the accident that took his life—one from Eagle Harbor Range keeper Henry Pierce (dated May 19) and one from Gull Rock assistant keeper James Corgan (dated May 22). Pierce wrote: "Reuben Hart left Copper Harbor at 8 a.m. for this station alone in his own sailboat a good one with wind SSE and blowing a good fresh breeze. He made several stretches coming down passed [*sic*] Gull Rock about 4 p.m. and lay to at two mile point of isle. He seemed to be engaged in fixing something around the boat for over one half an hour, he being observed by Mr. Corgan, Assistant Keeper at Gull Rock. He was next seen by his assistants Mr. Henry Fergeson and John Gustafson."

Hart seemed to have significant trouble navigating his boat around the island, the winds blowing him in and out, up and down, with not much aid from shore. He got as close as about five hundred feet when things took yet another turn for the worse, as Pierce noted.

"Mr. Hart appeared and climbed onto the uppermost part of the boat and divested himself of his outer clothing and motioned his two assts. They standing by the boathouse door at the time. They made a pusillanimous attempt to get the LH boat out of the boat house, but Fergeson 1st Asst. refused to assist Gustafson 2nd Asst. to get her more than partially out of the house, saying they could not to go him, saying they could not handle the boat, although begged by Gustafson to make an attempt to save the life of their principal. But no, he would not. He allowed him to drift past and away from them, imploring them by signs to come to him. He was so close that the two assts. ran out onto the rocks in an attempt to throw him a rope. They saw him over two hours afterward, when lighting the lamp still clinging to the uppermost fragment of the boat and flowing and diving toward the Canadian shore."

The lack of competency and compassion from the two assistant keepers did not go unnoticed by other nearby keepers, as referenced by Pierce. "To think of the suffering of that poor man drifting to his doom, with the two men he had chosen [as assistants] in plain sight to aid him in his lonely task of keeping this station, and they standing idly by and see him for hours drifting hopelessly away to a death. I cannot think of it that it doesn't make my flesh creep."

Corgan, who came from a long line of lighthouse keepers, was also appalled by the behavior of the men. "Assistants utterly incapable and wish to leave the station immediately," he said, and subsequently, he "commenced making endeavors to get two men to go to the island with me, for I have no desire to keep the company of those incompetent cowards." Neither Ferguson nor Gustafson found lighthouse employment after their brief stints at Manitou Island.

When an explosion rocked the **Stannard Rock Lighthouse**, twenty-four miles from the eastern shore of the Keweenaw Peninsula, around 9:30 p.m. on Sunday, June 18, 1961, one man was left missing (and presumed dead), one was severely injured and two others were left with bumps and bruises. It would be days before they were rescued from this 1882 lighthouse.

Head Keeper William A. Maxwell, thirty-five, was listed as an engineer first class with the U.S. Coast Guard. He was a married father of four from Houghton. After the explosion, he was never seen again.

Oscar R. Daniels Jr., twenty-three, suffered burns to his face, chest and arms, as well gashes on his left leg from a door that was blown loose and crushed against his lower body. Daniels, an electrician's mate, had only arrived at the light the day before to work on the generator.

The other two guardsmen, who suffered from exposure and other minor injuries, were eighteen-year-old Richard M. Horne and twenty-two-year-old Walter E. Scobie.

An article in the *Chicago Tribune* on June 22, 1961, noted: "The survivors said they thought the blast was due to explosion of 1,100 gallons of gasoline stored as generator fuel, but they had no theory as to the cause of the explosion. They said the resulting fire cut them off from supplies of food and clothing. All were wearing lightweight summer uniforms, inadequate for the cold Lake Superior nights. They managed to salvage two cans of beans, they said. These beans had been their only food thru three nights and two days—a period exceeding sixty hours. Fumes from the fire in the tower drove them off the structure, they said. They managed to take a strip of tarpaulin with them and used the canvas as both bed and tent in the camp they improvised on the pier."

That same day, an article in the *Detroit Free Press* indicated that Maxwell was working on the generator, preparing the light for automation the following year, when the explosion occurred. With all of the gasoline and coal housed in the lower level, it created plenty of fuel for the fire to burn for hours.

The blast forced flames up the stairwell and blew out the communication system, meaning there was no way for the men to reach out for help. It also knocked their twelve-foot-long dinghy into the lake, where it drifted away in the current. Horne made an attempt to swim after it, but the 40-degree-Fahrenheit water impacted his efforts, and he had to be rescued by Scobie, who threw a life ring into the water several times before pulling his coworker to safety.

A June 18, 1961 explosion at the Stannard Rock Lighthouse in Lake Superior left one man dead and three men stranded until they were finally rescued by the coast guard cutter *Woodrush*. *Courtesy of the U.S. Coast Guard.*

The three men were finally rescued by the cutter *Woodrush*, skippered by Lieutenant Commander C.G. Porter, around 11:30 p.m. on the Tuesday following the accident. Porter reported smoke was still emitting from the top of the seventy-eight-foot-tall tower, as the fire was still smoldering in the coal bunkers in the base of the tower more than two days later.

The **Big Bay Point Lighthouse** was tended by William H. Prior (also sometimes printed Pryor) during its first five years, from 1891 until his death in 1901.

One of his assistant keepers was none other than his nineteen-year-old son, George Edward (also noted as Edward George). The two worked together for about fifteen months before George fell on the steps of the crib, cutting his shin down to the bone. The young man was taken to the hospital in Marquette for treatment, but unfortunately, infection and gangrene set in, resulting in his death on June 13, 1901. George was buried in the Holy Cross Catholic Cemetery in Marquette.

William didn't take his son's death well, and he slipped into a state of depression. He was reportedly last seen on June 28, heading into the woods near the lighthouse with strychnine and his gun. The following November (eighteen months later), the *Sault Ste. Marie Evening News* published an article that said a deer hunter came upon a human skeleton hanging from a nearby tree. Police suspected it was Prior, given the tufts of red hair and remnants of a keeper's uniform found on the body. Since his death was ruled a suicide, Prior's remains could not be buried in the Catholic cemetery near his son (and rest of his family), and the exact location of his interment is unknown.

For more on this story, check out chapter 6 of *Michigan's Haunted Lighthouses*.

AUTHOR'S NOTE

This manuscript is a compilation of historical dates and other information from a variety of sources, including firsthand accounts. While the details are not always consistent, what is printed here represents an honest attempt to relay the facts or accounts as accurately as possible. Theories are based on timelines for the given lighthouses and keepers and are noted as such.

RESOURCES

Great Lakes Lighthouse Keepers Association
www.gllka.com

Friends of Dick Moehl Society
www.moehlmemorial.org

Seeing the Light: Lighthouses of the Western Great Lakes
www.terrypepper.com

United States Lighthouse Society
www.archives.uslhs.org

United States Coast Guard
www.uscg.mil

National Archives
www.archives.gov

Library of Congress
www.loc.gov

Ontario Historical Society
www.ontariohistoricalsociety.ca

Historical Society of Michigan
www.hsmichigan.org

Library of Michigan
www.michigan.gov/libraryofmichigan

Michigan State Archives
www.seekingmichigan.org

Michiganology
www.michiganology.org

Pure Michigan
www.michigan.org

West Michigan Tourist Association
www.wmta.org

Upper Peninsula Tourism and Recreation Association
www.uptravel.com

Promote Michigan
www.promotemichigan.com

Michigan's Haunted Lighthouses
www.mihauntedlighthouses.com

Wisconsin Maritime Museum
www.wisconsinmaritime.org

Lake Ontario

1. Gibraltar Point Lighthouse

City of Toronto
www.toronto.ca

Toronto Historical Society
www.torontohistory.net

Eamonn O'Keeffe Blog
www.1812andallthat.wordpress.com

Toronto Island Ferry
www.torontoisland.com/ferry.php

Lake Erie

2. South Bass Island Lighthouse

Put-in-Bay, Ohio
www.putinbay.com
www.visitputinbay.org

South Bass Island Lighthouse
www.ohioseagrant.osu.edu

Lake Erie Islands Historical Society
www.leihs.org

Miller Ferry
www.millerferry.com

Jet Express Ferry
www.jet-express.com

Lake Huron

3. Clapperton Island Lighthouse

Ontario Historical Society
www.ontariohistoricalsociety.ca

Manitoulin History Facebook Group
www.facebook.com/groups/manitoulinhistory/

LAKE MICHIGAN

4. St. Helena Island Lighthouse (and Other Straits of Mackinac Lights)

St. Helena Island Lighthouse
www.gllka.org/st-helena-island-light-station

White Shoal Light Historic Preservation Society
www.preservewhiteshoal.org

Old Mackinac Point Lighthouse—Mackinac State Historic Parks (Lake Huron)
www.mackinacparks.com

Spectacle Reef Preservation Society (Lake Huron)
www.spectaclereef.org

DeTour Reef Light Preservation Society (Lake Huron)
www.drlps.com

Ugly Ann Boat Tours
www.mackinawtour.com

5. Poverty Island Lighthouse

Visit Escanaba
www.visitescanaba.com

Delta County Historical Society
www.deltahistorical.org

6. Sand Point Lighthouse

U.S. Coast Guard
www.history.uscg.mil

7. Pilot Island Lighthouse

Friends of Plum and Pilot Islands
www.plumandpilot.org

Green Bay National Wildlife Refuge
www.fws.gov/refuge/green_bay

Door County Maritime Museum
www.dcmm.org

Washington Island Chamber of Commerce
www.washingtonisland.com

Destination Door County
www.doorcounty.com

8. Grosse Point Lighthouse

Grosse Point Lighthouse
www.grossepointlighthouse.net

Saugatuck Douglas Historical Society
www.sdhistoricalsociety.org

Manitou Islands Memorial Society
www.manitouislandsmemorialsociety.org

LAKE SUPERIOR

9. Grand Island Lighthouse

Alger County Historical Society
www.facebook.com/algerchs/

Munising Visitors Bureau
www.munising.org
Pictured Rocks National Lakeshore
www.nps.gov/piro/index.htm

Hiawatha National Forest—Munising
www.fs.usda.gov

10. Pie Island Lighthouse

Thunder Bay Museum
www.thunderbaymuseum.com

Fort William First Nation
www.fwfn.com

11. St. Ignace Lighthouse

Bowman Island Lodge and Charters
www.bowmanislandcharters.com

12. Michipicoten Island Lighthouse

Naturally Superior
www.naturallysuperior.com

Rock Island Lodge
www.rockislandlodge.ca

ABOUT THE AUTHOR

Dianna Higgs Stampfler has been writing professionally since her junior year at Plainwell High School, when she was also a reporter for a local weekly newspaper. By her senior year, she had her own column in that paper, was serving as news editor of her award-winning school newspaper and was also working in the newsroom at a local radio station (following in the footsteps of her father, who was a DJ for nearly sixty years before retiring in 2021).

She graduated from Western Michigan University with a dual degree in English with an emphasis in community journalism and communications with an emphasis in broadcasting. Dianna went on to work in public relations at Otsego Public Schools, where she also launched a middle school and elementary student newspaper program. Within four years, she was advising one of the top middle school papers in the state of Michigan, until she was forced out following a highly publicized case involving First Amendment issues and her student journalists.

In 1997, Dianna began working in Michigan's tourism industry, promoting destinations within a forty-one-county region at the West Michigan Tourist Association. In 2004, she launched Promote Michigan (PromoteMichigan.com), a public relations consulting company specializing in the hospitality, tourism, agriculture, culinary, natural resources, recreation, history and culture industries. It is her lifelong passion to share the stories of the people, places and products of Michigan and the Great Lakes region.

Over the past twenty-five-plus years, Dianna has penned countless articles for publications, such as *Pure Michigan Travel Ideas*, *Michigan Blue Magazine*, *Michigan Home & Lifestyle Magazine*, *Women's Lifestyle*, *AAA Living*, *West Michigan Carefree Travel*, *Lake Michigan Circle Tour & Lighthouse Guide*, *Lakeland Boating*, *Michigan Meetings + Events* and countless others.

In 2019, her first book, *Michigan's Haunted Lighthouses*, was published by The History Press and made it as far as becoming no. 2 in the Amazon.com rankings for haunted titles. It has recently been adapted for young readers as part of The History Press's Spooky America series. Dianna's latest book, *Death & Lighthouses on the Great Lakes: A History of Murder & Misfortune*, blends her passions for maritime history, dark tourism and true crime.